821.1 BAR

OXFORD
UNIVERSITY PRESS

Great Clarendon Street, Oxford OX2 6DP

Oxford University Press is a department of the University of Oxford.
It furthers the University's objective of excellence in research, scholarship,
and education by publishing worldwide in

Oxford   New York

Auckland   Cape Town   Dar es Salaam   Hong Kong   Karachi
Kuala Lumpur   Madrid   Melbourne   Mexico City   Nairobi
New Delhi   Shanghai   Taipei   Toronto

With offices in

Argentina   Austria   Brazil   Chile   Czech Republic   France   Greece
Guatemala   Hungary   Italy   Japan   South Korea   Poland   Portugal
Singapore   Switzerland   Thailand   Turkey   Ukraine   Vietnam

Oxford is a registered trade mark of Oxford University Press
in the UK and in certain other countries

Text reproduced courtesy of Oxford World's Classics

British Library Cataloguing in Publication Data
Data available

ISBN: 978-019-838687 2
10 9 8 7 6 5 4

Typeset in India by TNQ

Printed in Great Britain by CPI Antony Rowe, Chippenham

Paper used in the production of this book is a natural, recyclable product made
from wood grown in sustainable forests. The manufacturing process conforms
to the environmental regulations of the country of origin.

Contents

Introduction: English Literature

Unit F663 is the examined unit for English Literature A2, and carries 60% of the marks at A2. This text has been prescribed for Section B of the examination, where you are required to explore connections and comparisons between a drama text and a poetry text. In this introduction, you will find advice to help you prepare for the examination and the ways in which your work will be assessed.

Choice of texts

For Section B study, there is a choice of four drama texts and four poetry texts; your teacher will select one text from each group of four. There is a free choice of pairings of texts, and your teacher will look for connections between the texts he or she chooses. For example, there may be similarities of tone (e.g. humorous or heroic) or of subject matter (e.g. religious faith or the treatment of women). When you are preparing for the examination, it will be important to ensure that you know the individual texts in detail, and also that you have considered very thoroughly the possible connections and comparisons between them.

How to approach the examination

There will be a choice of six questions of which you can choose any one, regardless of your choice of set texts. These questions will ask about a central idea (e.g. power, or tragedy, or the role of women), and ask you to compare the treatment of this idea in your chosen texts.

For example, an essay question might read:

> By comparing one poetry and one drama text you have studied, discuss ways in which writers explore the dangers and delights of ambition.

The question begins by asking for comparison. You should understand this as an invitation to look for any similarities or differences, or any other connections between the two texts which help you to answer the question (see AO3 below). Most questions will ask you to look at 'ways in which' the writer treats the area under discussion; this part of the question directs you to consider the variety of approaches and methods used by writers in their treatment of the central theme or idea (see AO2 below). It is important to look carefully at the way the question is worded: in the question currently under discussion, for example, you are not just invited to discuss the theme of 'ambition' – you are asked to consider 'the <u>dangers and delights</u> of ambition'. To receive high marks, therefore, you need to consider carefully and explicitly both the destabilising and the rewarding qualities of ambition in your answer.

In an English Literature examination, there is never just one correct way to answer the question; however, there are some useful techniques which may help you to maximise your marks. It is helpful to write a short introduction to your essay which addresses the central idea in the question and relates it briefly to the texts you have chosen. The main body of your essay should include detailed discussion of the central idea, relating it to both of your set texts. You should ensure that you give the two texts roughly equal space in your answer, and that you include passages of sustained comparison: answers which deal with the two texts separately – perhaps with some perfunctory comparison by way of conclusion – will limit the marks they can achieve for looking at 'connections and comparisons' (see AO3 below). Finally, you should consider writing a conclusion which expresses succinctly the most important similarities and/or differences between your two texts in relation to the central idea in the question.

You should aim to use quotations to support your answer, especially with reference to AO2 (see below). Remember that AO2 can also be satisfied by more general references to the text, however, so that your own brief account of an event or moment in the text will sometimes be as helpful as a quotation.

What are the Assessment Objectives?

Your examiner will mark your work on the basis of four

Assessment Objectives (AO1, AO2, AO3 and AO4); the marking will be weighted in favour of AO3 and AO4.

Assessment Objective 1

> Articulate **creative**, **informed** and **relevant** responses to literary texts, using **appropriate terminology and concepts**, and **coherent, accurate written expression**.

Answers should be **creative** in the sense that good candidates will respond imaginatively, selecting and combining interesting and telling moments from the poetry and drama texts which help to arrive at an answer to the question.

They should be **informed** by a reasonable level of awareness concerning the set texts; for example, of information about the writers, the nature of poems or plays of the period in question and of poetry and drama in general. Such information should support the answer but not be allowed to dominate it.

Above all, answers should be **relevant**: when writing practice essays, it can be helpful to check every sentence to ensure that it is helping to form an answer to the question. You should aim to use key terms from the question at times during your essay, and especially in the conclusion.

During your study of your set texts, you should become familiar with **appropriate terminology and concepts**: for example, you should be able to discuss ideas such as 'dramatic irony' and 'metaphor'.

Coherent, accurate written expression is an essential part of a good answer: you should check the accuracy of your spelling and punctuation and especially your grammar to ensure that your essay is completed to a high standard and can be readily understood.

Assessment Objective 2

> Demonstrate **detailed critical understanding** in **analysing** the ways in which **structure, form and language** shape meanings in literary texts.

This Assessment Objective requires you to look closely at the detail of your set texts. You need to show how the writer of your poem or play achieves his or her effects through choices of language, form and structure. Methods of writing will vary according to the text you are studying: comments on **language** might include references to allusion (e.g. Pope's use of classical reference in *The Rape of the Lock*) or dialogue (e.g. polite conversation in *The School for Scandal*). Writing about **form** might lead you to consider choices the writer has made within his or her chosen genre (aspects of the revenge tragedy in *The Duchess of Malfi*, for example, or the use of the sonnet form in John Donne). Material relating to **structure** might focus on a writer's use of contrasting passages (e.g. scenes in *Dr Faustus* dealing with Faustus's enjoyments and those with his damnation, or Milton's use of narrative and dialogue in *Paradise Lost*). Remember, it is not enough to list methods used by a writer, even if you offer examples; you must always analyse the effects of the writing as well.

Assessment Objective 3

> **Explore connections and comparisons between different literary texts**, informed by interpretations of other readers.

This Assessment Objective combines different ideas, and here the main requirement is that you should **explore connections and comparisons** between your poetry and drama texts. During your answer, you should ensure that you offer some detailed and sustained comparison to show how the poet and the playwright you have studied compare in their treatment of the theme or idea in the question. You might find differences or similarities in the attitudes revealed in the text, or in the techniques used to express ideas (if you compare techniques, you will find that you are responding to AO2 and AO3 at the same time). You will find it helpful to bear in mind important features of the genre in which each text has been written. You can also receive credit for evidence that your answer is informed by **interpretations of other readers**, but this aspect of AO3 is of secondary importance in this section of the paper.

Assessment Objective 4

> Demonstrate understanding of the significance and influence of the **contexts** in which literary texts are written and received.

This Assessment Objective requires you to think about ideas and information in addition to the set texts. These ideas might be social or historical (e.g. what was the role of women in society at the time your text is written or is set?); they could be literary (what is this text like in relation to others by the same writer, or by his or her contemporaries?); they could be biographical (what were the important influences on the life of the writer when he or she produced this work?). It is also helpful to consider different critical reactions to the text over the period of time since its publication – or, in the case of drama, the performance history of your chosen play. In this part of the exam, it will be especially helpful to consider your set texts in the context of the genre in which they were written (see 'Cross-genre Comparison' below). Contextual study requires some research and learning, but should never be allowed to dominate an answer; take care to avoid writing long paragraphs of contextual information which do not support your argument.

Cross-genre Comparison

One of the most demanding aspects of this section is the requirement for 'cross-genre comparison'. At AS level, you will have covered techniques for comparison of two texts in Task 2 of your coursework unit; however, these texts may well have been from the same genre, so that you were comparing like with like. In Section B of F663, as in your A2 coursework, you are required to compare texts from different genres: here, poetry and drama, and, in your coursework, poetry and prose. For this reason, you will find it especially helpful to investigate and discuss characteristics of the genres of your chosen texts, and to use this study as part of the basis for your comparison. You might wish to ask yourself some of the following questions about the texts you are studying:

- What are the chief characteristics of drama? (Think about characters, action, dialogue, conflict, the role of the audience, etc.)
- What are the chief characteristics of poetry? (Think about form, imagery, concentration of linguistic effect, etc.)
- How 'poetic' is my drama text? (Is it written completely or partly in verse? Does the writer make significant use of poetic techniques such as elaborate similes or couplets?)
- How 'dramatic' is my poetry text? (Does it have a narrative line? Characters? A strong speaking voice? Does it include passages which deal with action or conflict? Does it lend itself to performance?)
- Why might a poet and a dramatist treat an idea or a theme in a different way? What are the constraints and opportunities offered by these different genres?

If you can supply detailed answers to these questions, preferably with textual support (detailed references or quotations), you will have completed some very effective preparation for this part of the exam. You may also like to use an appropriately adapted version of these questions to support your A2 coursework preparation; it certainly makes sense to be aware of the similarities of these two tasks, so that you can transfer the skills you learn between them.

OCR Specification Excerpt

The OCR GCE specification for English Literature is the document on which assessment is based; it specifies the content and skills to be covered in delivering a course of study. At all times, therefore, these excerpts should be read in conjunction with the specification. If clarification on a particular point is needed then reference should be in the first instance to the specification.

Unit Content

A2 Unit F663: *Drama and Poetry pre-1800* (Closed text)

There are two sections to this unit:

- Section A: Shakespeare
- *Section B: Drama and Poetry pre-1800*

Section B: Drama and Poetry pre-1800

This section requires candidates to explore contrasts, connections and comparisons between different literary texts. In their answers candidates must refer to **one drama text** and **one poetry text** from the lists of texts set for this section.

There will be a choice of six different questions each with a different focus. Candidates must select **one** question, and base their answer on a comparative study, with substantial discussion of both texts.

Candidates are required to show critical understanding in analysing ways in which structure, form and language shape meaning and demonstrate understanding of the significance and influence of the contexts in which literary texts are written and understood.

Advanced GCE Scheme of Assessment

A2 Unit F663: Drama and Poetry pre-1800

30% of the total Advanced GCE marks
2 h written paper 60 marks

Section B: Drama and Poetry pre-1800

Candidates are required to write an essay that is a comparative study of one drama and one poetry text.

Candidates are assessed on:

AO1: articulate creative, informed and relevant responses to literary texts, using appropriate terminology and concepts, and coherent, accurate written expression;

AO2: demonstrate detailed critical understanding in analysing the ways in which structure, form and language shape meanings in literary texts;

AO3: explore connections and comparisons between different literary texts, informed by interpretations of other readers;

AO4: demonstrate understanding of the significance and influence of the contexts in which literary texts are written and received.

The Pardoner's Tale

Assessment Criteria for A2 Unit F663: *Drama and Poetry pre-1800*

Band 6 26–30 marks	AO 1	• excellent and consistently detailed understanding of texts and question; • consistently fluent, precise writing in appropriate register; • critical terminology used accurately and consistently; • well-structured, coherent and detailed argument consistently developed.
	AO 2	• well-developed and consistently detailed discussion of effects (including dramatic effects) of language, form and structure; • excellent and consistently effective use of analytical methods; • consistently effective use of quotations and references to text, critically addressed, blended into discussion.
	AO 3	• excellent and consistently detailed comparative analysis of relationships between texts; • well-informed and effective exploration of different readings of text.
	AO 4	• consistently well-developed and consistently detailed understanding of the significance and influence of contexts in which literary texts are written and understood, as appropriate to the question.
Band 5 21–25 marks	AO 1	• good and secure understanding of texts and question; • good level of coherence and accuracy in writing, in appropriate register; • critical terminology used accurately; • well-structured argument with clear line of development.
	AO 2	• developed and good level of detail in discussion of effects (including dramatic effects) of language, form and structure; • good use of analytical methods; • good use of quotations and references to text, generally critically addressed.
	AO 3	• good, clear comparative analysis of relationships between texts; • judgements informed by recognition of different readings of texts.
	AO 4	• good, clear evaluation of the significance and influence of contexts in which literary texts are written and understood, as appropriate to the question.

Band 4 16–20 marks	AO 1	• competent understanding of texts and question; • clear writing in generally appropriate register; • critical terminology used appropriately; • straightforward arguments generally competently structured.
	AO 2	• generally developed discussion of effects (including dramatic effects) of language, form and structure; • competent use of analytical methods; • competent use of illustrative quotations and references to support discussion.
	AO 3	• competent comparative discussion of relationships between texts; • answer informed by some reference to different readings of texts.
	AO 4	• competent understanding of the significance and influence of contexts in which literary texts are written and understood, as appropriate to the question.
Band 3 11–15 marks	AO 1	• some understanding of texts and main elements of question; • some clear writing, some inconsistencies in register; • some appropriate use of critical terminology; • some structured argument evident, lacking development and/or full illustration.
	AO 2	• some attempt to develop discussion of effects (including dramatic effects) of language, form and structure; • some attempt at using analytical methods; • some use of quotations/references as illustration.
	AO 3	• some attempt to develop comparative discussion of relationships between texts; • some awareness of different readings of texts.
	AO 4	• some understanding of the significance and influence of contexts in which literary texts are written and understood, as appropriate to the question.

Band 2 **6–10** **marks**	AO 1	• limited understanding of texts and partial attempt at question; • inconsistent writing, frequent instances of technical error, limited use of appropriate register; • limited use of critical terminology; • limited attempt to structure discussion; tendency to lose track of argument.
	AO 2	• limited discussion of effects (including dramatic effects) of language, form and structure; • descriptive or narrative comment; limited use of analytical methods; • limited or inconsistent use of quotations, uncritically presented.
	AO 3	• limited comparative discussion of relationships between texts; • limited awareness of different readings of texts.
	AO 4	• limited understanding of the significance and influence of contexts in which literary texts are written and understood, as appropriate to the question.
Band 1 **0–5** **marks**	AO 1	• very little or no relevant understanding of texts; • very inconsistent writing with persistent serious technical errors, very little or no use of appropriate register; • persistently inaccurate or no use of critical terminology; • undeveloped, very fragmentary discussion.
	AO 2	• very little relevant or no discussion of effects (including dramatic effects) of language, form and structure; • very infrequent commentary; very little or no use of analytical methods; • very few quotations (eg one or two) used (and likely to be incorrect), or no quotations used.
	AO 3	• very little or no relevant comparative discussion of relationships between texts; • very little or no relevant awareness of different readings of texts.
	AO 4	• very little reference to (and likely to be irrelevant) or no understanding of the significance and influence of contexts in which literary texts are written and understood, as appropriate to the question.

The Pardoner's Tale

The Pardoner's portrait:
General Prologue

<blockquote>

With hym ther rood a gentil PARDONER

670   Of Rouncivale, his freend and his compeer,
That streight was comen fro the court of Rome.
Ful loude he soong 'Com hider, love, to me!'
This Somonour bar to hym a stif burdoun;
Was nevere trompe of half so greet a soun.

675   This Pardoner hadde heer as yelow as wex,
But smothe it heeng as dooth a strike of flex;
By ounces henge his lokkes that he hadde,
And therwith he his shuldres overspradde;
But thynne it lay, by colpons oon and oon.

680   But hood, for jolitee, wered he noon,
For it was trussed up in his walet.
Hym thoughte he rood al of the newe jet;
Dischevelee, save his cappe, he rood al bare.
Swiche glarynge eyen hadde he as an hare.

685   A vernycle hadde he sowed upon his cappe.
His walet, biforn hym in his lappe,
Bretful of pardoun comen from Rome al hoot.
A voys he hadde as smal as hath a goot.
No berd hadde he, ne nevere sholde have;

690   As smothe it was as it were late shave.
I trowe he were a geldyng or a mare.
But of his craft, fro Berwyk into Ware
Ne was ther swich another pardoner.
For in his male he hadde a pilwe-beer,

695   Which that he seyde was Oure Lady veyl;
He seyde he hadde a gobet of the seyl

</blockquote>

That Seint Peter hadde, whan that he wente
Upon the see, til Jhesu Crist hym hente.
He hadde a croys of latoun ful of stones,
700　And in a glas he hadde pigges bones.
But with thise relikes, whan that he fond
A povre person dwellynge upon lond,
Upon a day he gat hym moore moneye
Than that the person gat in monthes tweye;
705　And thus, with feyned flaterye and japes,
He made the person and the peple his apes.
But trewely to tellen atte laste,
He was in chirche a noble ecclesiaste.
Wel koude he rede a lessoun or a storie,
710　But alderbest he song an offertorie;
For wel he wiste, whan that song was songe,
He moste preche and wel affile his tonge
To wynne silver, as he ful wel koude;
Therefore he song the murierly and loude.

The Introduction to the Pardoner's Tale

The wordes of the Hoost to the Phisicien and the Pardoner.

　　Oure Hooste gan to swere as he were wood;
'Harrow!' quod he, 'by nayles and by blood!
This was a fals cherl and a fals justise.
As shameful deeth as herte may devyse
5　Come to thise juges and hire advocatz!
Algate this sely mayde is slayn, allas!
Allas, to deere boughte she beautee!
Wherfore I seye al day that men may see
That yiftes of Fortune and of Nature

10 Been cause of deeth to many a creature.
Hire beautee was hire deth, I dar wel sayn.
Allas, so pitously as she was slayn!
Of bothe yiftes that I speke of now
Men han ful ofte moore for harm than prow.
15 But trewely, myn owene maister deere,
This is a pitous tale for to heere.
But nathelees, passe over; is no fors.
I pray to God so save thy gentil cors,
And eek thyne urynals and thy jurdones,
20 Thyn ypocras, and eek thy galiones,
And every boyste ful of thy letuarie;
God blesse hem, and oure lady Seinte Marie!
So moot I theen, thou art a propre man,
And lyk a prelat, by Seint Ronyan!
25 Seyde I nat wel? I kan nat speke in terme;
But wel I woot thou doost myn herte to erme,
That I almoost have caught a cardynacle.
By corpus bones! but I have triacle,
Or elles a draughte of moyste and corny ale,
30 Or but I heere anon a myrie tale,
Myn herte is lost for pitee of this mayde.
Thou beel amy, thou Pardoner,' he sayde,
'Telle us som myrthe or japes right anon.'
        'It shal be doon,' quod he, 'by Seint Ronyon!
35 But first,' quod he, 'heere at this alestake
I wol bothe drynke and eten of a cake.'
        But right anon thise gentils gonne to crye,
'Nay, lat hym telle us of no ribaudye!
Telle us som moral thyng, that we may leere
40 Som wit, and thanne wol we gladly heere.'
        'I graunte, ywis,' quod he, 'but I moot thynke
Upon som honest thyng while that I drynke.'

The Pardoner's Prologue

Heere folweth the Prologe of the Pardoners Tale.

Radix malorum est Cupiditas. Ad Thimotheum, 6.

'Lordynges,' quod he, 'in chirches whan I
preche,
I peyne me to han an hauteyn speche,
45 And rynge it out as round as gooth a belle,
For I kan al by rote that I telle.
My theme is alwey oon, and evere was –
Radix malorum est Cupiditas.
'First I pronounce whennes that I come,
50 And thanne my bulles shewe I, alle and some.
Oure lige lordes seel on my patente,
That shewe I first, my body to warente,
That no man be so boold, ne preest ne clerk,
Me to destourbe of Cristes hooly werk.
55 And after that thanne telle I forth my tales;
Bulles of popes and of cardynales,
Of patriarkes and bishopes I shewe,
And in Latyn I speke a wordes fewe,
To saffron with my predicacioun,
60 And for to stire hem to devocioun.
Thanne shewe I forth my longe cristal stones,
Ycrammed ful of cloutes and of bones –
Relikes been they, as wenen they echoon.
Thanne have I in latoun a sholder-boon
65 Which that was of an hooly Jewes sheep.
"Goode men," I seye, "taak of my wordes keep;
If that this boon be wasshe in any welle,
If cow, or calf, or sheep, or oxe swelle
That any worm hath ete, or worm ystonge,
70 Taak water of that welle and wassh his tonge,

4

And it is hool anon; and forthermoore,
Of pokkes and of scabbe, and every soore
Shal every sheep be hool that of this welle
Drynketh a draughte. Taak kep eek what I telle:
75 If that the good-man that the beestes oweth
Wol every wyke, er that the cok hym croweth,
Fastynge, drynken of this welle a draughte,
As thilke hooly Jew oure eldres taughte,
His beestes and his stoor shal multiplie.
80   '"And, sires, also it heeleth jalousie;
For though a man be falle in jalous rage,
Lat maken with this water his potage,
And nevere shal he moore his wyf mystriste,
Though he the soothe of hir defaute wiste,
85 Al had she taken prestes two or thre.
        '"Heere is a miteyn eek, that ye may se.
He that his hand wol putte in this mitayn,
He shal have multipliyng of his grayn,
Whan he hath sowen, be it whete or otes,
90 So that he offre pens, or elles grotes.
            '"Goode men and wommen, o thyng warne
                I yow:
If any wight be in this chirche now
That hath doon synne horrible, that he
Dar nat, for shame, of it yshryven be,
95 Or any womman, be she yong or old,
That hath ymaked hir housbonde cokewold,
Swich folk shal have no power ne no grace
To offren to my relikes in this place.
And whoso fyndeth hym out of swich blame,
100 He wol come up and offre a Goddes name,
And I assoille him by the auctoritee
Which that by bulle ygraunted was to me."
            'By this gaude have I wonne, yeer by yeer,

An hundred mark sith I was pardoner.
105   I stonde lyk a clerk in my pulpet,
     And whan the lewed peple is doun yset,
     I preche so as ye han herd bifoore
     And telle an hundred false japes moore.
     Thanne peyne I me to strecche forth the nekke,
110   And est and west upon the peple I bekke,
     As dooth a dowve sittynge on a berne.
     Myne handes and my tonge goon so yerne
     That it is joye to se my bisynesse.
     Of avarice and of swich cursednesse
115   Is al my prechyng, for to make hem free
     To yeven hir pens, and namely unto me.
     For myn entente is nat but for to wynne,
     And nothyng for correccioun of synne.
     I rekke nevere, whan that they been beryed,
120   Though that hir soules goon a-blakeberyed!
     For certes, many a predicacioun
     Comth ofte tyme of yvel entencioun;
     Som for plesance of folk and flaterye,
     To been avaunced by ypocrisye,
125   And som for veyne glorie, and som for hate.
     For whan I dar noon oother weyes debate,
     Thanne wol I stynge hym with my tonge smerte
     In prechyng, so that he shal nat asterte
     To been defamed falsly, if that he
130   Hath trespased to my bretheren or to me.
     For though I telle noght his propre name,
     Men shal wel knowe that it is the same,
     By signes, and by othere circumstances.
     Thus quyte I folk that doon us displesances;
135   Thus spitte I out my venym under hewe
     Of hoolynesse, to semen hooly and trewe.
         'But shortly myn entente I wol devyse:

I preche of no thyng but for coveityse.
Therfore my theme is yet, and evere was,
140   *Radix malorum est Cupiditas.*
Thus kan I preche agayn that same vice
Which that I use, and that is avarice.
But though myself be gilty in that synne,
Yet kan I maken oother folk to twynne
145   From avarice and soore to repente.
But that is nat my principal entente;
I preche nothyng but for coveitise.
Of this mateere it oghte ynogh suffise.
      'Thanne telle I hem ensamples many oon
150   Of olde stories longe tyme agoon.
For lewed peple loven tales olde;
Swiche thynges kan they wel reporte and holde.
What, trowe ye, that whiles I may preche,
And wynne gold and silver for I teche,
155   That I wol lyve in poverte wilfully?
Nay, nay, I thoghte it nevere, trewely!
For I wol preche and begge in sondry landes;
I wol nat do no labour with myne handes,
Ne make baskettes and lyve therby,
160   By cause I wol nat beggen ydelly.
I wol noon of the apostles countrefete;
I wol have moneie, wolle, chese, and whete,
Al were it yeven of the povereste page,
Or of the povereste wydwe in a village,
165   Al sholde hir children sterve for famyne.
Nay, I wol drynke licour of the vyne
And have a joly wenche in every toun.
But herkneth, lordynges, in conclusioun:
Youre likyng is that I shal telle a tale.
170   Now have I dronke a draughte of corny ale,
By God, I hope I shal yow telle a thyng

That shal by reson been at youre likyng.
For though myself be a ful vicious man,
A moral tale yet I yow telle kan,
175 Which I am wont to preche for to wynne.
Now hoold youre pees! My tale I wol bigynne.'

The Pardoner's Tale

Heere bigynneth the Pardoners Tale.

In Flaundres whilom was a compaignye
Of yonge folk that haunteden folye,
As riot, hasard, stywes, and tavernes,
180 Where as with harpes, lutes, and gyternes,
They daunce and pleyen at dees bothe day and
      nyght,
And eten also and drynken over hir myght,
Thurgh which they doon the devel sacrifise
Withinne that develes temple in cursed wise
185 By superfluytee abhomynable.
Hir othes been so grete and so dampnable
That it is grisly for to heere hem swere.
Oure blissed Lordes body they totere –
Hem thoughte that Jewes rente hym noght
      ynough –
190 And ech of hem at otheres synne lough.
And right anon thanne comen tombesteres
Fetys and smale, and yonge frutesteres,
Syngeres with harpes, baudes, wafereres,
Whiche been the verray develes officeres
195 To kyndle and blowe the fyr of lecherye,
That is annexed unto glotonye.
The hooly writ take I to my witnesse

That luxurie is in wyn and dronkenesse.
    Lo, how that dronken Looth, unkyndely,
200 Lay by his doghtres two, unwityngly;
So dronke he was, he nyste what he wroghte.
    Herodes, whoso wel the stories soghte,
Whan he of wyn was repleet at his feeste,
Right at his owene table he yaf his heeste
205 To sleen the Baptist John, ful giltelees.
    Senec seith a good word doutelees;
He seith he kan no difference fynde
Bitwix a man that is out of his mynde
And a man which that is dronkelewe,
210 But that woodnesse, yfallen in a shrewe,
Persevereth lenger than doth dronkenesse.
O glotonye, ful of cursednesse!
O cause first of oure confusioun!
O original of oure dampnacioun,
215 Til Crist hadde boght us with his blood agayn!
Lo, how deere, shortly for to sayn,
Aboght was thilke cursed vileynye!
Corrupt was al this world for glotonye.
    Adam oure fader, and his wyf also,
220 Fro Paradys to labour and to wo
Were dryven for that vice, it is no drede.
For whil that Adam fasted, as I rede,
He was in Paradys; and whan that he
Eet of the fruyt deffended on the tree,
225 Anon he was out cast to wo and peyne.
O glotonye, on thee wel oghte us pleyne!
O, wiste a man how manye maladyes
Folwen of excesse and of glotonyes,
He wolde been the moore mesurable
230 Of his diete, sittynge at his table.
Allas, the shorte throte, the tendre mouth,

Maketh that est and west and north and south,
In erthe, in eir, in water, men to swynke
To gete a glotoun deyntee mete and drynke!
235 Of this matiere, O Paul, wel kanstow trete:
'Mete unto wombe, and wombe eek unto mete,
Shal God destroyen bothe,' as Paulus seith.
Allas, a foul thyng is it, by my feith,
To seye this word, and fouler is the dede,
240 Whan man so drynketh of the white and rede
That of his throte he maketh his pryvee
Thurgh thilke cursed superfluitee.

The apostel wepyng seith ful pitously,
'Ther walken manye of whiche yow toold have I –
245 I seye it now wepyng, with pitous voys –
They been enemys of Cristes croys,
Of whiche the ende is deeth; wombe is hir god!'
O wombe! O bely! O stynkyng cod,
Fulfilled of dong and of corrupcioun!
250 At either ende of thee foul is the soun.
How greet labour and cost is thee to fynde!
Thise cookes, how they stampe, and streyne, and grynde,
And turnen substaunce into accident
To fulfille al thy likerous talent!
255 Out of the harde bones knokke they
The mary, for they caste noght awey
That may go thurgh the golet softe and swoote.
Of spicerie of leef, and bark, and roote
Shal been his sauce ymaked by delit,
260 To make hym yet a newer appetit.
But, certes, he that haunteth swiche delices
Is deed, whil that he lyveth in tho vices.

A lecherous thyng is wyn, and dronkenesse
Is ful of stryvyng and of wrecchednesse.

265 O dronke man, disfigured is thy face,
　　　Sour is thy breeth, foul artow to embrace,
　　　And thurgh thy dronke nose semeth the soun
　　　As though thou seydest ay 'Sampsoun, Sampsoun!'
　　　And yet, God woot, Sampsoun drank nevere no
　　　　　wyn.
270 Thou fallest as it were a styked swyn;
　　　Thy tonge is lost, and al thyn honeste cure,
　　　For dronkenesse is verray sepulture
　　　Of mannes wit and his discrecioun.
　　　In whom that drynke hath dominacioun
275 He kan no conseil kepe; it is no drede.
　　　Now kepe yow fro the white and fro the rede,
　　　And namely fro the white wyn of Lepe
　　　That is to selle in Fysshstrete or in Chepe.
　　　This wyn of Spaigne crepeth subtilly
280 In othere wynes, growynge faste by,
　　　Of which ther ryseth swich fumositee
　　　That whan a man hath dronken draughtes thre,
　　　And weneth that he be at hoom in Chepe,
　　　He is in Spaigne, right at the toune of Lepe –
285 Nat at the Rochele, ne at Burdeux toun –
　　　And thanne wol he seye 'Sampsoun, Sampsoun!'
　　　　　　But herkneth, lordynges, o word, I yow
　　　　　　　　preye,
　　　That alle the sovereyn actes, dar I seye,
　　　Of victories in the Olde Testament,
290 Thurgh verray God, that is omnipotent,
　　　Were doon in abstinence and in preyere.
　　　Looketh the Bible, and ther ye may it leere.
　　　　　　Looke, Attilla, the grete conquerour,
　　　Deyde in his sleep, with shame and dishonour,
295 Bledynge ay at his nose in dronkenesse.
　　　A capitayn sholde lyve in sobrenesse.

And over al this, avyseth yow right wel
What was comaunded unto Lamuel –
Nat Samuel, but Lamuel, seye I;
300 Redeth the Bible, and fynde it expresly
Of wyn-yevyng to hem that han justise.
Namoore of this, for it may wel suffise.

And now that I have spoken of glotonye,
Now wol I yow deffenden hasardrye.
305 Hasard is verray mooder of lesynges,
And of deceite, and cursed forswerynges,
Blaspheme of Crist, manslaughtre, and wast also
Of catel and of tyme; and forthermo,
It is repreeve and contrarie of honour
310 For to ben holde a commune hasardour.
And ever the hyer he is of estaat,
The moore is he yholden desolaat.
If that a prynce useth hasardrye,
In alle governaunce and policye
315 He is, as by commune opinioun,
Yholde the lasse in reputacioun.

Stilboun, that was a wys embassadour,
Was sent to Corynthe in ful greet honour
Fro Lacidomye to make hire alliaunce.
320 And whan he cam, hym happede, par chaunce,
That alle the gretteste that were of that lond,
Pleyynge atte hasard he hem fond.
For which, as soone as it myghte be,
He stal hym hoom agayn to his contree,
325 And seyde, 'Ther wol I nat lese my name,
Ne I wol nat take on me so greet defame,
Yow for to allie unto none hasardours.
Sendeth othere wise embassadours;
For, by my trouthe, me were levere dye
330 Than I yow sholde to hasardours allye.

For ye, that been so glorious in honours,
Shul nat allyen yow with hasardours
As by my wyl, ne as by my tretee.'
This wise philosophre, thus seyde hee.

335   Looke eek that to the kyng Demetrius
The kyng of Parthes, as the book seith us,
Sente him a paire of dees of gold in scorn,
For he hadde used hasard ther-biforn;
For which he heeld his glorie or his renoun

340   At no value or reputacioun.
Lordes may fynden oother maner pley
Honest ynough to dryve the day awey.
    Now wol I speke of othes false and grete
A word or two, as olde bookes trete.

345   Gret sweryng is a thyng abhominable,
And fals sweryng is yet moore reprevable.
The heighe God forbad sweryng at al,
Witnesse on Mathew; but in special
Of sweryng seith the hooly Jeremye,

350   'Thou shalt swere sooth thyne othes, and nat lye,
And swere in doom and eek in rightwisnesse';
But ydel sweryng is a cursednesse.
Bihoold and se that in the firste table
Of heighe Goddes heestes honurable,

355   Hou that the seconde heeste of hym is this:
'Take nat my name in ydel or amys.'
Lo, rather he forbedeth swich sweryng
Than homycide or many a cursed thyng;
I seye that, as by ordre, thus it stondeth;

360   This knoweth, that his heestes understondeth,
How that the seconde heeste of God is that.
And forther over, I wol thee telle al plat
That vengeance shal nat parten from his hous
That of his othes is to outrageous.

365 'By Goddes precious herte,' and 'By his nayles,'
And 'By the blood of Crist that is in Hayles,
Sevene is my chaunce, and thyn is cynk and
    treye!'
'By Goddes armes, if thou falsly pleye,
This daggere shal thurghout thyn herte go!' –
370 This fruyt cometh of the bicched bones two,
Forsweryng, ire, falsnesse, homycide.
Now, for the love of Crist, that for us dyde,
Lete youre othes, bothe grete and smale.
But, sires, now wol I telle forth my tale.

375   Thise riotoures thre of whiche I telle,
Longe erst er prime rong of any belle,
Were set hem in a taverne to drynke,
And as they sat, they herde a belle clynke
Biforn a cors, was caried to his grave.
380 That oon of hem gan callen to his knave:
'Go bet,' quod he, 'and axe redily
What cors is this that passeth heer forby;
And looke that thou reporte his name weel.'
        'Sire,' quod this boy, 'it nedeth never-a-deel;
385 It was me toold er ye cam heer two houres.
He was, pardee, an old felawe of youres,
And sodeynly he was yslayn to-nyght,
Fordronke, as he sat on his bench upright.
Ther cam a privee theef men clepeth Deeth,
390 That in this contree al the peple sleeth,
And with his spere he smoot his herte atwo,
And wente his wey withouten wordes mo.
He hath a thousand slayn this pestilence.
And, maister, er ye come in his presence,
395 Me thynketh that it were necessarie
For to be war of swich an adversarie.
Beth redy for to meete hym everemoore;

Thus taughte me my dame; I sey namoore.'
'By Seinte Marie!' seyde this taverner,
400 'The child seith sooth, for he hath slayn this yeer,
Henne over a mile, withinne a greet village,
Bothe man and womman, child, and hyne, and
     page;
I trowe his habitacioun be there.
To been avysed greet wysdom it were,
405 Er that he dide a man a dishonour.'
     'Ye, Goddes armes!' quod this riotour,
'Is it swich peril with hym for to meete?
I shal hym seke by wey and eek by strete,
I make avow to Goddes digne bones!
410 Herkneth, felawes, we thre been al ones;
Lat ech of us holde up his hand til oother,
And ech of us bicomen otheres brother,
And we wol sleen this false traytour Deeth.
He shal be slayn, he that so manye sleeth,
415 By Goddes dignitee, er it be nyght!'
     Togidres han thise thre hir trouthes plight
To lyve and dyen ech of hem for oother,
As though he were his owene ybore brother.
And up they stirte, al dronken in this rage,
420 And forth they goon towardes that village
Of which the taverner hadde spoke biforn.
And many a grisly ooth thanne han they sworn,
And Cristes blessed body they torente –
Deeth shal be deed, if that they may hym hente!
425   Whan they han goon nat fully half a mile,
Right as they wolde han troden over a stile,
An oold man and a povre with hem mette.
This olde man ful mekely hem grette,
And seyde thus, 'Now, lordes, God yow see!'
430   The proudeste of thise riotoures three

Answerde agayn, 'What, carl, with sory grace!
Why artow al forwrapped save thy face?
Why lyvestow so longe in so greet age?'
       This olde man gan looke in his visage,
435 And seyde thus: 'For I ne kan nat fynde
A man, though that I walked into Ynde,
Neither in citee ne in no village,
That wolde chaunge his youthe for myn age;
And therfore moot I han myn age stille,
440 As longe tyme as it is Goddes wille.
Ne Deeth, allas, ne wol nat han my lyf.
Thus walke I, lyk a resteless kaityf,
And on the ground, which is my moodres gate,
I knokke with my staf, bothe erly and late,
445 And seye "Leeve mooder, leet me in!
Lo how I vanysshe, flessh, and blood, and skyn!
Allas, whan shul my bones been at reste?
Mooder, with yow wolde I chaunge my cheste
That in my chambre longe tyme hath be,
450 Ye, for an heyre clowt to wrappe me!"
But yet to me she wol nat do that grace,
For which ful pale and welked is my face.
       'But, sires, to yow it is no curteisye
To speken to an old man vileynye,
455 But he trespasse in word or elles in dede.
In Hooly Writ ye may yourself wel rede:
"Agayns an oold man, hoor upon his heed,
Ye sholde arise;" wherfore I yeve yow reed,
Ne dooth unto an oold man noon harm now,
460 Namoore than that ye wolde men did to yow
In age, if that ye so longe abyde.
And God be with yow, where ye go or ryde!
I moot go thider as I have to go.'
       'Nay, olde cherl, by God, thou shalt nat so,'

465 Seyde this oother hasardour anon;
'Thou partest nat so lightly, by Seint John!
Thou spak right now of thilke traytour Deeth.
That in this contree alle oure freendes sleeth.
Have heer my trouthe, as thou art his espye,
470 Telle where he is or thou shalt it abye,
By God and by the hooly sacrement!
For soothly thou art oon of his assent
To sleen us yonge folk, thou false theef!'
        'Now, sires,' quod he, 'if that yow be so leef
475 To fynde Deeth, turne up this croked wey,
For in that grove I lafte hym, by my fey,
Under a tree, and there he wole abyde;
Noght for youre boost he wole him no thyng
        hyde.
Se ye that ook? Right there ye shal hym fynde.
480 God save yow, that boghte agayn mankynde,
And yow amende!' Thus seyde this olde man;
And everich of thise riotoures ran
Til he cam to that tree, and ther they founde
Of floryns fyne of gold ycoyned rounde
485 Wel ny an eighte busshels, as hem thoughte.
No lenger thanne after Deeth they soughte,
But ech of hem so glad was of that sighte,
For that the floryns been so faire and brighte,
That doun they sette hem by this precious hoord.
490 The worste of hem, he spak the firste word.
        'Bretheren,' quod he, 'taak kep what that I
                eye;
My wit is greet, though that I bourde and pleye.
This tresor hath Fortune unto us yiven
In myrthe and joliftee oure lyf to lyven,
495 And lightly as it comth, so wol we spende.
Ey, Goddes precious dignitee! Who wende
To-day that we sholde han so fair a grace?

But myghte this gold be caried fro this place
Hoom to myn hous, or elles unto youres –
500 For wel ye woot that al this gold is oures –
Thanne were we in heigh felicitee.
But trewely, by daye it may nat bee.
Men wolde seyn that we were theves stronge,
And for oure owene tresor doon us honge.
505 This tresor moste ycaried be by nyghte
As wisely and as slyly as it myghte.
Wherfore I rede that cut among us alle
Be drawe, and lat se wher the cut wol falle;
And he that hath the cut with herte blithe
510 Shal renne to the town, and that ful swithe,
And brynge us breed and wyn ful prively.
And two of us shul kepen subtilly
This tresor wel; and if he wol nat tarie,
Whan it is nyght, we wol this tresor carie,
515 By oon assent, where as us thynketh best.'
That oon of hem the cut broghte in his fest,
And bad hem drawe and looke where it wol falle;
And it fil on the yongeste of hem alle,
And forth toward the toun he wente anon.
520 And also soone as that he was gon,
That oon of hem spak thus unto that oother:
'Thow knowest wel thou art my sworen brother;
Thy profit wol I telle thee anon.
Thou woost wel that oure felawe is agon.
525 And heere is gold, and that ful greet plentee,
That shal departed been among us thre.
But nathelees, if I kan shape it so
That it departed were among us two,
Hadde I nat doon a freendes torn to thee?'
530 That oother answerde, 'I noot hou that may
        be.

He woot that the gold is with us tweye;
What shal we doon? What shal we to hym seye?'
        'Shal it be conseil?' seyde the firste shrewe,
'And I shal tellen in a wordes fewe
535 What we shal doon, and brynge it wel aboute.'
        'I graunte,' quod that oother, 'out of doute,
That, by my trouthe, I wol thee nat biwreye.'
        'Now,' quod the firste, 'thou woost wel we
                be tweye,
And two of us shul strenger be than oon.
540 Looke whan that he is set, that right anoon
Arys as though thou woldest with hym pleye,
And I shal ryve hym thurgh the sydes tweye
Whil that thou strogelest with hym as in game,
And with thy daggere looke thou do the same;
545 And thanne shal al this gold departed be,
My deere freend, bitwixen me and thee.
Thanne may we bothe oure lustes all fulfille,
And pleye at dees right at oure owene wille.'
And thus acorded been thise shrewes tweye
550 To sleen the thridde, as ye han herd me seye.
        This yongeste, which that wente to the toun,
Ful ofte in herte he rolleth up and doun
The beautee of thise floryns newe and brighte.
'O Lord!' quod he, 'if so were that I myghte
555 Have al this tresor to myself allone,
Ther is no man that lyveth under the trone
Of God that sholde lyve so murye as I!'
And atte laste the feend, oure enemy,
Putte in his thought that he sholde poyson
                beye,
560 With which he myghte sleen his felawes tweye;
For-why the feend foond hym in swich lyvynge
That he hadde leve him to sorwe brynge.

For this was outrely his fulle entente,
To sleen hem bothe and nevere to repente.
565   And forth he gooth, no lenger wolde he tarie,
Into the toun, unto a pothecarie,
And preyde hym that he hym wolde selle
Som poyson, that he myghte his rattes quelle;
And eek ther was a polcat in his hawe,
570   That, as he seyde, his capouns hadde yslawe,
And fayn he wolde wreke hym, if he myghte,
On vermyn that destroyed hym by nyghte.
The pothecarie answerde, 'And thou shalt have
A thyng that, also God my soule save,
575   In al this world ther is no creature
That eten or dronken hath of this confiture
Noght but the montance of a corn of whete,
That he ne shal his lif anon forlete;
Ye, sterve he shal, and that in lasse while
580   Than thou wolt goon a paas nat but a mile,
This poysoun is so strong and violent.'
This cursed man hath in his hond yhent
This poysoun in a box, and sith he ran
Into the nexte strete unto a man,
585   And borwed [of] hym large botelles thre,
And in the two his poyson poured he;
The thridde he kepte clene for his drynke.
For al the nyght he shoop hym for to swynke
In cariynge of the gold out of that place.
590   And whan this riotour, with sory grace,
Hadde filled with wyn his grete botels thre,
To his felawes agayn repaireth he.
What nedeth it to sermone of it moore?
For right as they hadde cast his deeth bifoore,
595   Right so they han hym slayn, and that anon.

And whan that this was doon, thus spak that
    oon:
'Now lat us sitte and drynke, and make us merie,
And afterward we wol his body berie.'
And with that word it happed hym, par cas,

600   To take the botel ther the poyson was,
And drank, and yaf his felawe drynke also,
For which anon they storven bothe two.
       But certes, I suppose that Avycen
Wroot nevere in no canon, ne in no fen,

605   Mo wonder signes of empoisonyng
Than hadde thise wrecches two, er hir endyng.
Thus ended been thise homycides two,
And eek the false empoysonere also.
       O cursed synne of alle cursednesse!

610   O traytours homycide, O wikkednesse!
O glotonye, luxurie, and hasardrye!
Thou blasphemour of Crist with vileynye
And othes grete, of usage and of pride!
Allas, mankynde, how may it bitide

615   That to thy creatour, which that the wroghte
And with his precious herte-blood thee boghte,
Thou art so fals and so unkynde, allas?
       Now, goode men, God foryeve yow youre
         trespas,
And ware yow fro the synne of avarice!

620   Myn hooly pardoun may yow alle warice,
So that ye offre nobles or sterlynges,
Or elles silver broches, spoones, rynges.
Boweth youre heed under this hooly bulle!
Cometh up, ye wyves, offreth of youre wolle!

625   Youre names I entre heer in my rolle anon;
Into the blisse of hevene shul ye gon.
I yow assoille, by myn heigh power,

Yow that wol offre, as clene and eek as cleer
As ye were born. – And lo, sires, thus I preche.
630 And Jhesu Crist, that is oure soules leche,
So graunte yow his pardoun to receyve,
For that is best; I wol yow nat deceyve.
        But, sires, o word forgat I in my tale:
I have relikes and pardoun in my male,
635 As faire as any man in Engelond,
Whiche were me yeven by the popes hond.
If any of yow wole, of devocion,
Offren and han myn absolucion,
Com forth anon, and kneleth heere adoun,
640 And mekely receyveth my pardoun;
Or elles taketh pardoun as ye wende,
Al newe and fressh at every miles ende,
So that ye offren, alwey newe and newe,
Nobles or pens, whiche that be goode and trewe.
645 It is an honour to everich that is heer
That ye mowe have a suffisant pardoneer
T'assoille yow in contree as ye ryde,
For aventures whiche that may bityde.
Paraventure ther may fallen oon or two
650 Doun of his hors and breke his nekke atwo.
Looke which a seuretee is it to yow alle
That I am in youre felaweshipe yfalle,
That may assoille yow, bothe moore and lasse,
Whan that the soule shal fro the body passe.
655 I rede that oure Hoost heere shal bigynne,
For he is moost envoluped in synne.
Com forth, sire Hoost, and offre first anon,
And thou shalt kisse the relikes everychon,
Ye, for a grote! Unbokele anon thy purs.'
660   'Nay, nay!' quod he, 'thanne have I Cristes
                curs!

Lat be,' quod he, 'it shal nat be, so theech!
Thou woldest make me kisse thyn olde breech,
And swere it were a relyk of a seint,
Though it were with thy fundement depeint!
665 But, by the croys which that Seint Eleyne fond,
I wolde I hadde thy coillons in myn hond
In stide of relikes or of seintuarie.
Lat kutte hem of, I wol thee helpe hem carie;
They shul be shryned in an hogges toord!'
670   This Pardoner answerde nat a word;
So wrooth he was, no word ne wolde he seye.
    'Now,' quod oure Hoost, 'I wol no lenger
      pleye
With thee, ne with noon oother angry man.'
But right anon the worthy Knyght bigan,
675 Whan that he saugh that al the peple lough,
'Namoore of this, for it is right ynough!
Sire Pardoner, be glad and myrie of cheere;
And ye, sire Hoost, that been to me so deere,
I prey yow that ye kisse the Pardoner.
680 And Pardoner, I prey thee, drawe thee neer,
And, as we diden, lat us laughe and pleye.'
Anon they kiste, and ryden forth hir weye.

Heere is ended the Pardoners Tale

Notes

The Pardoner's portrait: General Prologue

In *The General Prologue* Chaucer gives a description of each of the pilgrims, sometimes hinting at aspects of their character. The Pardoner rides with another disreputable member of the party, the Summoner. The description of the Pardoner follows that of the Summoner, who is another official of the Church. His job is to summon wrongdoers to the Church courts. He is as corrupt as the Pardoner and, like the Pardoner, he exploits his position using blackmail and extortion to line his own pockets.

The Pardoner has yellow hair spread over his shoulders, and he rides bare-headed except for a little cap. He has glaring eyes and a voice as small as a goat's. He has just returned from Rome and has with him a bag full of pardons. He has no beard and is not likely to grow one; the narrator comments that he thinks the Pardoner is 'a gelding or a mare', that is, not a virile man. In terms of skill at doing his job, there is no one to match him between Berwick and Ware. In his bag he has a pillow case, which he says is the Virgin Mary's veil, and other bogus religious relics. He says, however, that he can earn more money in a day with these relics than a poor country parson can earn in two months.

669   **hym**   the Summoner.
670   **Rouncivale**   the hospital of the Blessed Virgin Mary at Charing Cross. The order was originally founded in Roncesvalles in France.
      compeer   companion.
672   **Com hider, love, to me!**   a line from a popular song. Note its worldly rather than spiritual implications.
673   **bar to hym a stif burdoun**   sang along with him in a deep bass.
674   **trompe**   trumpet.
676   **strike of flex**   hank of flax (the implication being that it is dry and lifeless).

677 **ounces** bunches of rats' tails. Clerics were not supposed to have long hair and so this reflects the Pardoner's disregard of the rules.

679 **colpons oon and oon** wisps here and there (again contributing to the unattractive picture of the Pardoner).

680 **for jolitee** for comfort (a suggestion that he wants to show off his long hair).

682 **al of the newe jet** in the latest fashion (again emphasizing the Pardoner's vanity).

683 **Dischevelee** hair untidy.

684 **Swiche glarynge... an hare** note the further unattractive details and the animal comparison. Staring eyes were often associated with licentiousness.

685 **vernycle** a copy of the handkerchief of St Veronica, with which she is supposed to have wiped Christ's face on his way to crucifixion. It was a sign of having made a pilgrimage to Rome.

687 **Bretful** brimful.

688 **as smal as hath a goot** as small as a goat's (i.e. thin and bleating). Goats were also traditionally lecherous.

689–91 **No berd... or a mare** Chaucer seems to be implying a kind of sterility or impotence. Perhaps this is the physical equivalent of his spiritual sterility. What overall impression does this physical description of the Pardoner give you so far?

694 **male** pouch or bag.
pilwe-beer pillow case.

696 **gobet of the seyl** piece of the sail.

697–8 **That Seint Peter... hym hente** St Peter was a fisherman before he was called by Jesus as a disciple. This is another of the Pardoner's 'sales' ploys to impress his audience with the rarity and religious significance of his relics.

699 **croys of latoun ful of stones** latoun is an alloy of tin and copper which is gold coloured but is, in fact, base metal. The gems in it would also be false, perhaps symbolic of the falsity of the Pardoner himself.

700 **pigges bones** presumably he would claim these were of important religious significance.

702 **person** parson.

705–6 **flaterye and japes... his apes** with false flattery and tricks he made fools of the parson and the people (i.e. his congregation).

707 **atte laste**   finally.
708 **a noble ecclesiaste**   a splendid cleric. Do you think Chaucer
means us to take this at face value?
710 **alderbest**   best of all.
song an offertorie   the part of the religious service where
members of the congregation offer bread and wine to the priest.
712 **affile**   polish up (the implication being that he is a smooth talker).

The words of the Host to the Physician and the Pardoner: Lines 1–42

The Physician has just finished his tale, which entails the death of
a beautiful young girl. She is killed by her own father in order to
prevent her being sexually exploited by a wicked judge. In
response to this tale, the Host begins to swear and condemn the
treacherous and villainous judge. He observes, sadly, that the
maiden paid a high price for her beauty. He tells the other
pilgrims that unless he gets a good drink of strong ale or hears a
cheerful story straightaway, he will be overwhelmed with feelings
of pity for this girl. He calls upon the Pardoner to tell some jokes
or something light-hearted. The Pardoner says that he will do so,
but first he needs a drink and something to eat. The rest of them
cry out that they don't want him to tell them anything coarse,
but something moral so that they can learn some wisdom. He
agrees and says he will think about what story to tell them while
he is having his drink.

1-2 **gan to swere... by blood!**   the Host began to swear as if he
were mad (the nails are those of the cross and the blood is of
Christ). The Host's use of blasphemous oaths here and later
creates an ironic link to one of the Pardoner's themes – that of
blasphemous swearing.
3 **justise**   judge or magistrate.
5 **thise juges**   such judges (i.e. false ones).
advocatz   advocates or lawyers.
6 **Algate**   all the same.

sely   innocent or blessed.

7 **to deere boughte she beautee**   she paid too high a price for her beauty.

9 **yiftes of Fortune and of Nature**   the gifts of wealth and prosperity, and of beauty and intelligence.

14 **han**   have.
prow   benefit or advantage.

15 **myn owene maister deere**   these words are addressed to the Physician.

17 **is no fors**   it doesn't matter.

18 **cors**   body.

19 **urynals and thy jurdones**   urinals and chamber-pots (physicians used urine to help diagnose a patient's illness).

20 **ypocras**   the Host seems to confuse 'ypocras', which was a spiced wine, with the name Hippocrates, the Greek physician who is often regarded as the 'father of medicine'.
galiones   perhaps a confusion for Galen, the second-century Greek physician. It is possible that both of these are malapropisms as the Host attempts to impress with his medical knowledge.

21 **boyste**   box.
letuarie   medicine.

23 **So moot I theen**   a phrase frequently found in Chaucer meaning something similar to the modern phrases 'upon my life' or 'as I live and breathe'.

24 **Seint Ronyan**   generally agreed to mean St Ninian. Perhaps another mistake on the part of the Host.

25 **I kan nat speke in terme**   I can't use your technical terms.

26 **erme**   grieve.

27 **cardynacle**   a 'cardiacle' was a heart attack. Perhaps Chaucer is providing the Host with another amusing malapropism here, suggesting a link with the word 'cardinal'.

28 **By corpus bones**   another oath: 'God's bones'.
triacle   remedy.

32 **beel amy**   good fellow (perhaps mock courtesy here using French, the language of court).

35 **alestake**   inn sign.

38 **ribaudye**   coarse, dirty jokes or story.

39 **leere**   learn.

27

The Pardoner begins his prologue: Lines 43–90

The Pardoner begins by describing to the company how he sets about preaching to his congregation, and he tries to make himself sound as impressive as possible. He tells them how he takes particular care to speak loudly and clearly, and he compares his voice to a bell ringing out resoundingly (45). He explains to them how he always preaches on the same theme – 'the love of money is the root of all evil' (48), and then goes on to describe the techniques that he uses to convince the simple people who make up his congregation of his power and influence. He begins by showing them official documents endorsed by the bishop which give him the authority to preach (50). His whole purpose here is to convince his audience of his credentials so that he can exploit their religious faith to line his own pocket. In order to convince them further, he speaks a few words in Latin and then shows them the religious relics that he possesses, and which he convinces the simple folk are scraps of cloth and bones belonging to saints and holy figures. He claims that these relics possess the power to cure illness and bring good fortune. His purpose, of course, is to sell these bogus articles to his gullible audience.

43 **Lordynges**   gentlemen.
44 **I peyne me**   I take the trouble.
   hauteyn   loud.
45 **as round as gooth a belle**   as clearly as a bell.
46 **by rote**   by heart.
48 *Radix malorum est Cupiditas*   the love of money is the root of all evil. The text the Pardoner uses for his preaching is from St Paul's First Epistle to Timothy, Chapter 6, Verse 10. This forms the moral base for the *Pardoner's Tale* and is particularly ironic as, although the Pardoner may preach this message, he certainly does not practise it himself.
49 **whennes that I come**   the *General Prologue* tells us that the Pardoner has just returned from Rome (which would add

weight to his religious credentials).

50 **bulles** official religious documents.
   alle and some each and every one of them.

51 **Oure lige lordes seel on my patente** the seal of the bishop
   licensing the Pardoner to preach.

52 **my body to warente** to protect myself.

53 **ne preest ne clerk** both of these were churchmen (unlike the
   Pardoner who was a layman). Ironically, he is implying that
   some churchmen might cast doubt on him.

54 **Me to destourbe of** to hinder me from.

56 **Bulles of popes and of cardynales** other 'official'
   documents. Do you think all the Pardoner's official papers and
   warrants are genuine?

57 **patriarkes** leading churchmen.

59 **To saffron with my predicacioun** to add colour to my
   preaching (saffron is used in cooking to provide colour to
   dishes).

61 **cristal stones** glass boxes containing the so-called religious
   relics (rags or cloth).

62 **cloutes** rags or cloth.

63 **as wenen they echoon** as everyone believes.

64 **in latoun** mounted in a brass-like alloy.

65 **an hooly Jewes sheep** a deliberately vague reference by the
   Pardoner to suggest an unnamed but important biblical figure –
   another of the Pardoner's ploys to impress his audience.

69 **That any worm hath ete, or worm ystonge** that has eaten
   some harmful creature or been bitten by a snake. ('Worm'
   suggests a snake, but was also used more generally to describe
   any kind of creeping animal or insect.)

71 **hool anon** recovers quickly.

72 **Of pokkes and of scabbe** pox and scab – skin diseases that
   sheep sometimes catch.

75 **good-man** head of the household.

76 **wyke** week.

79 **stoor** stock or possessions.

82 **potage** soup.

83–5 **And nevere shal he moore… prestes two or thre** he will
   never be jealous again even though he knew of his wife's
   misdeeds and she had two or three priests as her lovers. Note

the way in which the Pardoner keeps his audience's attention here. He touches on two popular topics of the times – the unfaithfulness of women and the promiscuity of priests.

86 **miteyn** a special mitten used for sowing seed by hand.
90 **grotes** groats – silver coins worth about four pence.

His tricks are very profitable: Lines 91–136

As a further encouragement to his congregation to buy his pardons, the Pardoner employs clever psychology. He suggests to them that those in the congregation who have committed terrible sins are too ashamed to confess them, and that any woman who has been unfaithful to her husband will not be able to make an offering for the Pardoner's relics (97). Those who have not committed such gross sins, though, can come forward with their offerings. Cleverly, the Pardoner makes it look as though those who do not make an offering have, perhaps, committed some terrible sin.

The Pardoner then boasts to the other pilgrims how he makes a large amount of money every year by using this trick (104). Far from being shamefaced about this, he prides himself on doing his work so effectively, and creates a picture for the other pilgrims of how he stands in his pulpit stretching forward to address his congregation as he preaches his deceitful stories (108). He is completely open with the other pilgrims about his one and only intention – he is interested in making money and is not at all concerned about the correction of sin (118). In fact, he does not care what happens to the souls of the members of his congregation after they have died (120).

He claims that many sermons are preached by people who have evil intentions, and he is clear that if anyone in his congregation has spoken ill of himself or other pardoners he will verbally attack them (127) but without naming them specifically.

Here he reveals a vindictive temperament, as well as another way in which he abuses his position.

92 **wight**   person.
93 **horrible**   terrible or outrageous. Suggests a stronger sense of something really bad than the word usually implies in modern English.
94 **yshryven**   confessed (which would involve the public exposure of lies).
96 **cokewold**   cuckold (a husband whose wife is unfaithful to him). Note the emphasis on sexual sin.
97 **grace**   divine or spiritual strength.
99 **whoso fyndeth hym out of swich blame**   anyone who feels they are free of sin.
101 **assoille**   absolve. Being a layman and not a priest, the Pardoner only had the power to grant pardons and not to absolve people of their sins. The Pardoner is assuming power that he does not have.
103 **gaude**   trick.
    wonne   gained or profited.
104 **An hundred mark**   a large sum of money in Chaucer's time. Notice how the Pardoner is completely unashamed of the amount of money he makes out of people. In fact, he boasts about it.
105 **I stonde lyk a clerk in my pulpet**   again the Pardoner presents himself as having the power of a priest.
106 **lewed peple**   uneducated, common people.
108 **false japes**   false or deceitful tricks.
109 **peyne I me to**   I take the trouble to.
110 **bekke**   nod.
111 **As dooth a dowve sittynge on a berne**   on one level a simile with a country image. In another way, however, the image of the Pardoner as a dove, the biblical symbol of love and peace, has an ironic edge to it.
112 **yerne**   quickly, busily.
113 **it is joye to se my bisynesse**   it is a pleasure to see me at my work. The Pardoner clearly has a high opinion of his own performance.
115 **free**   eager.

116 **yeven hir pens**   give their pennies.
117 **wynne**   to make a profit. The Pardoner's boasting leaves his
      audience in no doubt of the falsity of any spiritual dimension.
120 **hir soules goon a-blakeberyed**   literally, 'their souls go
      blackberrying' – an image of souls wandering about. The
      Pardoner is really saying that he couldn't care less if their souls
      are damned, once he has their money. Why do you think he
      uses this image?
121–2 **many a predicacioun… yvel entencioun**   many sermons are
      preached with evil intentions. Note the irony here: this is
      exactly what the Pardoner is doing – preaching sermons to
      make money out of people.
126 **For whan I dar noon oother weyes debate**   when I can find
      no other way to quarrel. He is prepared to use his tongue to
      attack those he cannot attack openly.
128 **asterte**   avoid or escape.
130 **trespased**   offended.
      bretheren   the Pardoner presents himself as part of a
      'brotherhood' of pardoners, which gives the impression of
      being part of a religious order. This is a deliberate ploy
      designed to impress and therefore deceive the members of the
      audience he intends to sell pardons to.
131 **propre**   own. Note here that this is another of the Pardoner's
      ploys. Although he cannot, of course, know who in his
      audience may have 'trespassed', he tries to make them believe
      he does, thus blackmailing them into being generous with their
      offerings.
133 **signes**   signs or hints.
134 **quyte**   repay or get even with.
      doon us displesances   do things that displease us.
135 **Thus spitte I out my venym**   note the metaphor here – the
      Pardoner creates an image of himself as a snake, a symbol often
      associated with deviousness, evil and the devil.
      hewe   colour or appearance.

The Pardoner reveals more about himself and his methods: Lines 137–176

The Pardoner reinforces the fact that his theme is always the same – 'the love of money is the root of all evil', but he freely admits that he is only interested in his own profit (138, 147). He seems to have no problem with the fact that he preaches against the very same sin that he is guilty of. He feels that, even though he is guilty of avarice, this does not mean that he cannot effectively persuade others to repent of that sin (144). However, he is quick to point out that any such positive outcome is only incidental to his main intent (146).

He then reveals to the pilgrims more of the tricks he uses at the expense of his congregation. These include telling them the old stories from the past that the simple, ignorant and uneducated people who make up his congregation enjoy so much and like to hold in their minds (152). The Pardoner then comments that the pilgrims surely don't seriously expect him to live in poverty when he can earn silver and gold by preaching (155). He tells them that he refuses to do manual work or beg for money (note his address to the pilgrims – he is completely frank about his own purposes). Nor will he copy the apostles, who lived simply, carrying out their good works. Instead he will take people's money or any goods that he can sell and convert into money.

We are left in no doubt of his completely unscrupulous nature when he tells them that he will take money from the poorest widow in the village even if it means her children starving (165). He wants to drink wine and have a lively woman in very town.

He ends his prologue by telling the pilgrims that now he has drunk some ale he will be able to tell them a tale to their liking. He says that even though he is a corrupt and wicked man, he is still able to tell them a moral tale – the one he usually preaches to make money from his congregation.

138 **coveityse** covetousness.

140 *Radix malorum est Cupiditas* the love of money is the root of all evil (from St Paul's First Epistle to Timothy, Chapter 6).

141–5 **Thus kan I... to repente** although the Pardoner is aware that he practises the same sin that he preaches against, he seems to believe that this enables him to persuade others to repent for it. Note the irony of this.

149 **ensamples** illustrative stories – often, in medieval sermons, stories were used as examples to support the main point or argument being made.

152 **reporte and holde** repeat and hold in their minds.

153 **trowe ye** think you – the Pardoner is using this in the sense of asking the other pilgrims 'you don't really think that... ?' He clearly is crediting his present audience with more sense than the audience he usually preaches to.

159 **Ne make baskettes** nor make baskets (a reference here to the little-known saint, St Paul the Hermit, who lived by making baskets, not the much more widely known St Paul the Apostle).

161 **countrefete** imitate. Although in preaching his sermons the Pardoner is imitating the apostles, his motives for doing so are very different.

162 **moneie, wolle, chese, and whete** if poor people cannot give him money, he is happy to take payment in kind.

163 **Al were it yeven of** even if it were given by.

165 **Al sholde hir children sterve for famyne** even if her children starve – the Pardoner is completely unashamed that he will take from the very poorest of people.

166 **Nay, I wol drynke licour of the vyne** note the juxtaposition of poverty and starvation with the image of the Pardoner enjoying the good things of life.

172 **by reson** if you are reasonable.

173 **though myself be a ful vicious man** though I am a very wicked man. Note the irony that although he is a completely immoral character, he can tell a moral tale.

175 **for to wynne** he gives a reminder of the purpose of his sermon. What do you think about the Pardoner from the things he has to say in this section?

The Pardoner sets the scene: Lines 177–211

The Pardoner sets the scene of his tale in Flanders, a country that had a reputation, in Chaucer's time, for heavy drinking and riotous living. He introduces the three young revellers, the *riotoures*, who are at the centre of his tale. These young men spend their whole time drinking, eating, gambling, swearing, and visiting brothels (179). He comments on the shockingly blasphemous oaths that they use so frequently and the disrespect that they show to Christ through this blasphemous swearing (187). To make matters worse, they just laugh at each other's sins. Female dancers, fruit and sweet-meat sellers, and prostitutes frequent the places these young men visit and the Pardoner says that all these people are agents of the devil whose purpose is to ignite the fires of lechery (195), a sin closely linked to gluttony.

The Pardoner uses the scriptures to support his claim that the sin of lechery is closely associated with wine and drunkenness. To further support this view, he uses the story of the drunken Lot (see note to line 199) and then refers to Herod's order to kill John the Baptist (see note to line 202). Significantly, though, he bends the truth in both these stories in order to make them support his argument more effectively. He also cites Seneca's view that there is no difference between a drunken man and a mad man, except madness lasts longer than drunkenness.

177 **Flaundres** Flanders (part of modern Belgium) – the Flemish had a reputation for heavy drinking in Chaucer's time.
whilom once, or 'once upon a time'. This opening placing the story in some vague time in the past is used to begin a number of *The Canterbury Tales*.
178 **haunteden** made a habit of or devoted themselves to.
folye foolishness or wrongdoing.
179 **riot, hasard, stywes** debauchery or loose living, gambling, brothels.
180 **gyternes** stringed instrument, an early version of a guitar.

181 **dees** dice.

182 **over hir myght** to excess.

183–4 **Thurgh which… develes temple** through which (behaviour) they make sacrifice to the devil within that devil's temple (the tavern). Here the Pardoner suggests that, through their debauchery and excess, they make the tavern a temple to the devil. The idea of the tavern as a place of sin is, of course, a well-known one.

185 **superfluytee abhomynable** disgusting or morally detestable excesses.

186 **othes** oaths or swearing.

188 **totere** tear in pieces.

189 **Hem thoughte… noght ynogh** the Pardoner is suggesting that the oaths, which used Christ's name, were such blasphemies that every one was like a re-crucifying of Christ. The reference to the Jews reflects the anti-Semitism of this period. In Chaucer's time, the Jews were blamed for the murder of Christ. They were persecuted extensively, and all Jews were expelled from England twice, in 1290 and 1306.

190 **lough** laughed.

191 **tombesteres** dancing girls.

192 **Fetys and smale** elegant and slim.
frutesteres female fruit-sellers (note the sexual image of temptation linked to the female and fruit).

193 **baudes** bawds or pimps.
wafereres women selling sweets and confectionery (often associated with acting as go-betweens in secret love affairs).

194 **develes officeres** servants or agents of the devil.

196 **annexed** linked.

197–8 **The hooly writ… wyn and dronkenesse** the Pardoner is making reference to St Paul's Epistle to the Ephesians, 5:18, which states 'And be not drunk with wine, wherein is excess'. Here he is following the pattern of the medieval sermon in using a biblical reference to support his point.

199 **dronken Looth** the Pardoner refers to the biblical story where Lot's daughters, knowing the shortage of men and wanting to have children, got him so drunk that he slept with them without realizing what he was doing.

202 **Herodes, whoso wel the stories soghte** Herod, as those who

look carefully at the scriptures will know. The Pardoner claims that Herod was drunk when he gave the order for the execution of John the Baptist. He is claiming to be an authority on the scriptures in such as way as to deny contradiction.

203 **Whan he of wyn was repleet** when he was full of wine. Again the Pardoner is distorting the story for his own ends. The Bible does not say that Herod was drunk.

204 **heeste** order.

205 **ful giltelees** although he was completely innocent.

206 **Senec** Seneca, a Roman writer, philosopher and dramatist in the first century AD. The Pardoner cites him as an authority.

210 **woodnesse** madness.
yfallen in a shrewe occurring in a scoundrel. What techniques has the Pardoner used in this section to make his argument more effective?

The Pardoner condemns gluttony: Lines 212–262

The Pardoner now launches into a full attack on the evils of gluttony. It is a sin of such magnitude that it was responsible for the original damnation of mankind, he claims, as it was Adam's greed that caused him to take the apple from Eve (222). This necessitated Christ sacrificing himself to redeem mankind – a high price to pay for the gluttony of Adam.

The Pardoner then goes on to create a vivid picture of the disgusting nature of gluttony. He does this by using a number of visual images, warning that if people knew the dangers of excess and gluttony they would be more moderate in eating and drinking. Again, the Pardoner uses the scriptures to support his point, saying that St Paul preached against gluttony (237) and creates a revolting image as he describes the stomach as a stinking bag full of dung and filth, with foul sounds being emitted from either end of the body (lines 248–250).

He concludes his attack on gluttony by pointing out the

labour and expense that goes into preparing food to satisfy gluttonous appetites, and warns that he who delights in the pleasures of gluttony is dead already as long as he continues with this sin (262).

212 **O glotonye**   with the Pardoner's use of the exclamation here and throughout his sermon, he is using a rhetorical technique (*apostrophe* in medieval rhetorical terms) employed in preaching. Its purpose is to draw attention to and emphasize the content.

213 **confusioun**   downfall or ruin.

215 **Til Crist... blood agayn**   till Christ redeemed us with his blood.

216 **deere**   at a high price.

219 **Adam oure fader**   the Pardoner links the idea of Adam eating the apple given to him by Eve, and therefore being cast out of the garden of Eden, with the idea of gluttony.

222 **as I rede**   I understand.

224 **the fruyt deffended**   the forbidden fruit.

226 **pleyne**   complain.

227 **wiste a man**   if a man knew.

231 **the shorte throte, the tendre mouth**   the Pardoner emphasizes how brief the pleasure gained from eating food is, which adds weight to the negative aspects of gluttony.

233 **swynke**   labour.

235 **wel kanstow trete**   you deal with this matter well.

236–7 **Mete unto... destroyen bothe**   the Pardoner is using a quotation from St Paul's First Epistle to the Corinthians, 6:13, 'Meat for the belly and the belly for meats'.

240 **white and rede**   white and red wine.

241 **pryvee**   latrine, lavatory (a particularly disgusting image).

242 **superfluitee**   excess.

243 **The apostel**   i.e. St Paul.

244 **walken**   behave.

247 **wombe is hir god**   whose belly is their god.

248 **O wombe! O bely! O stynkyng cod**   O stomach! O belly! O stinking bag. Note the repeated use of 'O' (*apostrophe*) and exclamation (*exclamatio*) as the Pardoner reaches the climax of this part of his sermon.

249 **corrupcioun**   decayed matter.
250 **At either… is the soun**   another unpleasant image used by the
   Pardoner to emphasize his point.
252 **streyne**   passing sauces etc. through strainers, but this also
   carries the connotation of working hard, straining themselves
   to produce dishes for the glutton.
253 **And turnen substaunce into accident**   the Pardoner is using
   medieval philosophical language to describe the art of cooking.
   Substance was the essential inward essence, and accident the
   outer appearance. The suggestion here is that cooking involves
   a kind of deception, often concealing what food contains or is
   made of. This is a reference to the Catholic Mass, where bread
   and wine is said to become the body and blood of Christ.
256 **mary**   marrow.
257 **golet**   gullet or throat.
259 **his sauce ymaked by delit**   his sauce is made for his delight.
260 **newer appetit**   keener appetite.
261 **haunteth**   make a habit of.
   delices   delights.
262 **lyveth**   devotes himself to. What impact does the Pardoner's
   use of imagery have in this section?

The Pardoner condemns drinking: Lines 263–302

The Pardoner now turns his attention to drinking and
drunkenness. He begins by creating a detailed picture of the
drunkard as a man with a disfigured face, bad breath, who is foul
to embrace and snores loudly (265–268). The drunkard stumbles
around like a stuck pig and loses the power of speech and a sense
of decency, and a drunken man cannot keep a secret.

The Pardoner then warns his audience against a particular
mixture of Spanish and French wines which is especially strong.
Once again the Pardoner uses the Bible to support his argument,
telling his audience how the victories described in the Old
Testament were achieved through abstinence and prayer

(288–291). He also uses the example of Attila the Hun, who supposedly died in his sleep after a bout of drunkenness (294). He concludes with a reference to the Book of Proverbs about Lemuel, who was also warned against drinking (298).

264 **stryvyng** quarrelling.
268 **Sampsoun, Sampsoun!** the Pardoner is using onomatopoeia to imitate the heavy snoring of a drunk.
269 **Sampsoun drank nevere no wyn** ironically, the biblical character epitomizing strength never drank wine.
270 **styked swyn** stuck pig.
271 **al thyn honeste cure** all your concern for honourable things.
272 **sepulture** burial or tomb.
273 **discrecioun** good sense or judgement.
274 **hath dominacioun** has taken a hold.
275 **conseil** secret.
276 **kepe yow fro** keep yourselves away from.
277 **white wyn of Lepe** a white wine from Lepe in north-east Spain.
278 **Fysshstrete or in Chepe** Fish Street and Cheapside, busy market areas in medieval London.
279–80 **This wyn of Spaigne... othere wynes** the wine of Lepe was used to dilute the more expensive French wines.
281 **fumositee** it was believed that fumes from alcohol in the stomach would go directly to the head and so cause drunkenness.
282–5 **That whan a man... Burdeux toun** when a man has drunk three draughts of this wine and when he is at home in Cheapside he will think that he is in Spain, at Lepe and not Rochelle or Bordeaux (French towns – the centre of French wine-making).
286 **And thanne wol he seye 'Sampsoun, Sampsoun!'** and then his snoring will begin (see line 268). Do you think the Pardoner's description of the effects of drink is realistic?
287–92 **But herkneth... it leere** note how the Pardoner changes the slant of his preaching here. Until now he has focused on the specific, physical effects of drink. He now broadens his message to claim that all the noble deeds and victories in the Old Testament, with the help of God, who is omnipotent, were

performed in abstinence and prayer.

288 **sovereyn**   noble.

290 **omnipotent**   all-powerful.

292 **leere**   learn.

293 **Looke**   take, for example; a conventional way to introduce an example (*exemplum*) in the medieval sermon.
Attilla   leader of the Huns and a powerful warlord and conqueror. Reputed to have died in his bed after a night of heavy drinking and debauchery.

297 **avyseth yow right wel**   consider carefully.

298 **Lamuel**   a reference to the Book of Proverbs, 31: 4–5, 'It is not for kings, O Lemuel, it is not for kings to drink wine; nor for princes strong drink: lest they drink, and forget the law, and pervert the judgement of any of the afflicted.' Note the Pardoner's use of another less well-known biblical figure to support his argument.

301 **wyn-yevyng**   the giving of wine.

The Pardoner attacks gambling: Lines 303–342

The Pardoner now moves on to attack gambling. He claims that gambling is the mother of lies and deceit, blasphemy and manslaughter and causes people to squander both their money and time. In addition, to be considered to be a gambler brings shame and dishonour, and the higher the rank of the gambler the worse he is considered to be. The Pardoner illustrates his point with a reference to Stilboun (see note to line 317) and to Demetrius (see note to line 335).

304 **I yow deffenden hasardrye**   I will, for your benefit, forbid you to gamble.

305 **mooder of lesynges**   mother of lies.

306 **cursed forswerynges**   perjury or the breaking of oaths.

308 **catel and of tyme**   property and time.

309 **repreeve**   shame.

310 **For to ben... hasardour**   to be considered a common gambler.

311–2 **And ever... yholden desolaat**   the greater his (the gambler's) status, the greater his disgrace.

313 **useth hasardrye**   makes a habit of gambling.

316 **reputacioun**   esteem.

317 **Stilboun**   an ambassador who was sent from Sparta to Corinth to make an alliance with the Corinthians. When he arrived he found the leaders of the city were gambling. As soon as he realized this he returned secretly to his own country, saying that he was not prepared to lose his reputation in Corinth, nor dishonour himself by making an alliance with gamblers. Chaucer would have been very familiar with this story, which he takes from *Policraticus*, a book written by the twelfth-century scholar John of Salisbury.

329 **me were levere dye**   I would rather die.

333 **As by my wyl, ne as by my tretee**   neither by my will nor any treaty of mine.

335 **kyng Demetrius**   the Pardoner uses another example (*exemplum*) here.

338 **ther-biforn**   previously.

342 **to dryve the day awey**   to pass the time. What do you notice about the kinds of examples that the Pardoner uses to condemn gambling?

The Pardoner condemns swearing: Lines 343–374

In the final part of his sermon, before he returns to his tale, the Pardoner condemns the swearing of oaths, another subject mentioned in ancient books. Again he uses several quotations from the Bible to support his attack (348–349). His argument is that 'oaths should be true and never lie', and that pointless swearing is a great wickedness. He goes on to make reference to the Ten Commandments to prove that taking the name of God in vain is an even greater sin than murder (see notes to lines 353–358).

The Pardoner then gives some examples of the type of oaths that he is condemning (365–369) and urges his audience to abandon the use of blasphemous oaths, whether they be trivial or great.

343 **othes**   oaths, i.e. swearing.

344 **as olde bookes trete**   as ancient books treat the subject.

346 **fals sweryng**   false swearing, i.e. swearing oaths with no intention of keeping them.
reprevable   blameworthy.

348 **Witnesse on Mathew**   call on St Matthew as a witness. The Pardoner is referring to Matthew, 5:33–4 here – 'Again, ye have heard that it hath been said by them of old time, Thou shalt not forswear thyself, but shalt perform unto the Lord thine oaths. But I say unto you, swear not at all.'

349 **hooly Jeremye**   the Pardoner now uses a quotation from the Old Testament prophet Jeremiah: 'And thou shalt swear, the Lord liveth, in truth, in judgement, and in righteousness' (4:2).

352 **ydel sweryng**   idle or pointless swearing.

353 **the firste table**   the first tablet of the law, i.e. the first five of the Ten Commandments given to Moses by God.

354 **Goddes heestes honurable**   God's honourable commandments.

355 **seconde heeste**   second commandment.

356 **'Take nat my name in ydel or amys'**   'Thou shalt not take my name in vain'.

357–8 **Lo, rather he… cursed thyng**   he forbids such swearing before killing or other wicked things.

359 **as by ordre, thus it stondeth**   this is the order in which it stands. The Pardoner is arguing that as the second commandment this comes before the commandment forbidding killing, and therefore is more important.

360 **his heestes understondeth**   he that knows his commandments. Why does the Pardoner make this comment?

362 **al plat**   all plainly.

363–4 **That vengeance… is to outrageous**   God's vengeance shall not leave the house of he whose oaths are outrageous.

366 **Hayles**   an abbey in Gloucestershire that claimed to have a phial containing Christ's blood.

43

367 **Sevene is my chaunce, and thyn is cynk and treye!** here the
Pardoner uses the language of medieval gambling. In the dice
game called hazard, *chaunce* was a throw which entitled the
thrower to another turn; *cynk* and *treye* are five and three on the
dice.

368 **falsly pleye** cheat.

370 **bicched** cursed.

bones two the two dice (dice were generally made of bone).

371 **ire** anger.

373 **Lete** forsake, put aside.

The Pardoner returns to his tale:
Lines 375–418

Having condemned the range of sins associated with the three
revellers, the Pardoner now returns to his tale. As the three are
drinking in a tavern they hear the bell signalling a burial. They
learn that an old friend of theirs has been killed by a stealthy
thief called Death. A serving boy warns them that the plague,
Death, has killed a thousand people and that the revellers should
approach him very warily.

The drunken revellers, however, determine to seek Death out
and kill him. The three of them pledge to live and die for one
another – an ironic touch bearing in mind what is to come.

375 **riotoures** revellers.

376 **erst er** before.

prime the first prayers of the day. The bell for these prayers
rang at 6 am. The point here is that the revellers are still
drinking in the early hours of the morning – an immediate
indicator of their dissolute lifestyle.

379 **Biforn a cors** the bell they hear is signalling a funeral. Note
how the idea of death is introduced early in the story.

380 **knave** servant, serving boy.

381 **bet** quickly.

axe redily ask quickly.

382 **heer forby**   past here.

384 **it nedeth never-a-deel**   there's no need for that.

385 **er ye cam heer two houres**   two hours before you came here.

386 **pardee**   by God, or indeed.

felawe   friend or companion.

388 **Fordronke**   very drunk.

389 **privee theef**   secret thief.

clepeth   call.

391–2 **And with his spere... withouten wordes mo**   with his spear he stabbed your friend through the heart and then went on his way without saying a word. Note the vivid personification of Death here. In Chaucer's time Death was often portrayed as a skeleton armed with a spear.

393 **this pestilence**   this plague (Death takes the form of the plague, very common in the Middle Ages.)

394 **his presence**   i.e. Death's presence.

395 **Me thynketh**   it seems to me.

397 **Beth redy... everemoore**   be ready to meet him at all times.

398 **dame**   mother. What impression is created by the boy?

401 **Henne over a mile**   over a mile from here.

402 **hyne, and page**   labourer and servant.

404–5 **To been... a dishonour**   It would be very wise to be careful before he does any harm to someone.

406 **'Ye, Goddes armes!'**   note the blasphemous oaths (and the others used here by the revellers – *Goddes digne bones!* (409), *Goddes dignitee* (415).

408 **by wey and eek by strete**   on every path and also road.

409 **digne**   holy.

410 **we thre been al ones**   we three are all one (the brotherhood between the three revellers is stressed).

411–2 **Lat ech of us holde up... otheres brother**   the holding up of hands is part of the formalizing of their fellowship. This adds to the irony in the light of subsequent events.

413 **this false traytour Deeth**   ironically they call Death the traitor.

416 **Togidres**   together.

hir trouthes plight   swore their oaths (further emphasis on the apparent bond between them).

417–8 **To lyve and dyen... ybore brother**   note once again the irony of these lines.

The revellers meet the old man: Lines 419–481

The revellers jump up in a drunken rage and head towards the village, swearing many blasphemous oaths as they go (422). The Pardoner re-emphasizes his point about such oaths tearing the body of Christ (see line 188).

After they have gone about half a mile they meet an old man who greets them humbly and politely. The proudest of the revellers returns the greeting rudely (note the contrast between the old man's manner and the rudeness and unpleasantness of the reveller). He asks the old man why he is so muffled up and why he has lived so long. The old man tells him that he cannot find anyone to exchange youth for his age, and so he must live for as long as God wills it. Even Death refuses to take his life. He rebukes the revellers for speaking so discourteously to him, and wants to be on his way. The young men, though, will not allow him to leave and insist that he tells them where Death is. He tells them that they will find him under a tree in a nearby grove. Despite the fact that they have treated him so rudely, he bids farewell to them politely. Note that he hopes that God will bless and redeem them and help them mend their ways (480–481).

419 **al dronken in this rage**   in this drunken, passionate anger.
    Notice the emphasis that the Pardoner places on the
    drunkenness of the revellers, a sin that he has already
    condemned.
422 **grisly**   terrible, horrible.
423 **Cristes blessed body they torente**   note the reference back to
    the idea of blasphemous oaths tearing Christ's body apart (line
    188). A contrast is created here between Christ's victory over
    death through his sacrifice on the cross and resurrection, and
    the revellers' confused and drunken notion of killing Death
    themselves.
424 **may hym hente**   can take him.
426 **troden over a stile**   climbed over a stile.

427 **An oold man... hem mette**   the man is 'old' and 'poor' and
therefore forms an immediate contrast to the revellers. On one
level he is a symbolic figure representing both goodness and
humility. However, neither his age nor his poverty gain him any
respect in the eyes of the young revellers.

428 **ful mekely**   humbly, politely. Note the emphasis on the old
man's humility.

429 **God yow see**   may God look after you.

430 **proudeste**   most arrogant. Note the contrast with the old
man's humility.

431 **What, carl, with sory grace**   what, fellow, bad luck to you (the
reveller's response to the old man is both sneering and rude).

432 **Why artow al forwrapped**   why are you completely wrapped up?

433 **lyvestow**   do you live.

434 **visage**   face.

436 **though that I walked into Ynde**   though I walked to India
(the same sense as 'to the ends of the earth').

439 **moot I han myn age stille**   I must keep my age permanently.

441 **Ne Deeth... my lyf**   nor will Death accept my life. (The irony
here is that the old man seeks Death but cannot die, whereas
the revellers seek to kill Death but die themselves.)

442 **kaityf**   wretch or prisoner.

443 **moodres gate**   mother's gate (the earth is his mother, and he
seeks the 'gate' to find his way back to her).

444 **I knokke with my staf**   i.e. as if knocking to find the gate to
leave this life and return to his mother, the earth.

445 **Leeve mooder**   dear mother (i.e. the earth).

446 **Lo how... skyn!**   graphic, visual imagery of the old man
wasting away.

448–50 **Mooder... wrappe me!**   Mother, I would exchange with you
the chest of clothes that has been in my room a long time for a
hair shroud to wrap me in. (The sense here is that the old man
wants to exchange life for death).

452 **welked**   withered or wrinkled.

453–63 **But, sires... have to go**   the old man supports his point with a
biblical reference from the Old Testament: 'Thou shalt rise up
before the hoary head, and honour the face of the old man, and
fear thy God' (Leviticus, 19:32).

457 **hoor upon his heed**   white haired (from the idea of 'hoar frost', a particularly intense, white frost).

458 **I yeve yow reed**   I can give you this advice.

459–61 **Ne dooth... longe abyde**   never do any more harm to an old man now than you would want people to do to you when you are old, if you live that long. (Note the irony in this comment.)

465 **this oother hasardour**   this other gambler.

466 **Thou partest nat so lightly**   you don't get away from us that easily.

469 **Have heer my trouthe**   take my word for it.
espye   spy.

470 **shalt it abye**   shall pay for it.

471 **By God and by the hooly sacrement!**   note the reveller's continued use of blasphemous oaths.

472 **oon of his assent**   in league with him.

474 **be so leef**   if it is so dear to you.

475 **turne up this croked wey**   take this crooked path. (Note the symbolic significance of the 'crooked path', i.e. the path of sin.)

476 **by my fey**   by my faith.

478 **Noght... hyde**   he will not hide because of your boast.

479 **ook**   oak tree. Note the emphasis placed on the setting here – *grove*, *tree* and *ook*. The tree was used in medieval art to symbolize the fall of Adam and Eve. Here the revellers' own demise begins in a place of trees.

480 **God save yow**   the old man blesses those who have treated him badly, saying he hopes that God will redeem them. Do you think the old man is just what he seems, or do you think he represents something more?

The revellers find the gold: Lines 482–550

The revellers run to the place that the old man has indicated and come to the tree. They do not find Death there, but they do find a large hoard of gold coins (484). They do not continue their search for Death after making this discovery, and are delighted with their find.

The worst of the revellers tells the others that Fortune has given them the treasure so that they can live a carefree, happy life (493–494). He knows, though, that it is important that they move the gold secretly to his house or one of the other revellers' houses. If they are seen with the gold, people will say they are thieves (503). They draw lots to see who should go to town to bring back food and drink while the other two keep guard over the treasure. The youngest of the revellers draws the short straw and he leaves for town.

As soon as he has gone, one reveller speaks to the other and suggests that they should split the gold between them. He outlines his plan to murder the third reveller when he returns from town (540–544).

484 **floryns**   gold coins (named after the city of Florence where they were first minted).

485 **eighte busshels**   a bushel was a measurement by volume. Here it emphasizes the large quantity of gold they found. (Note that they find the gold at the base of a tree – 'the love of money is the root of all evil').

490 **The worste of hem**   the worst of them. ('The most arrogant' spoke in line 430, and it is the 'youngest' of them who goes to town in line 518.)

491 **taak kep**   take notice, take heed.

492 **wit**   intelligence.
    bourde and pleye   joke and play around.

496 **Goddes precious dignitee**   another blasphemous oath.
    Who wende   who would have thought.

497 **fair a grace**   stroke of luck.

499 **to myn hous**   his first thought is that the gold is his.

500 **woot**   know.

501 **heigh felicitee**   great happiness (*felicitee* can be used to imply a 'blessed' state – ironical in the context here).

502 **by daye it may nat bee**   note the implication of dishonest dealing here – he recognizes that the gold cannot be moved in daylight.

503–4 **Men wolde seyn... us honge**   suddenly possessing so much money would attract suspicion. Notice that none of the revellers thinks of reporting their find or trying to find out whom it belongs to.

503 **stronge**   strong, dastardly.

504 **oure owene**   the assumption is that this treasure belongs to them.

506 **As wisely and as slyly as it myghte**   as cleverly and secretly as possible.

507–8 **I rede... Be drawe**   they will draw straws. (Note that the decision is based on chance – whoever draws the short straw will run to town.)

510 **renne**   run.

511 **breed and wyn**   bread and wine. (The body and blood of Christ are also implied).
  prively   secretly.

513 **tarie**   delay.

516 **fest**   fist.

523 **Thy profit**   something to your profit or advantage.

526 **departed**   divided.

527 **shape it**   arrange it.

529 **Hadde I... to thee?**   have I not done you a friendly turn?

530 **I noot hou that may be**   I don't know how that can be.

533 **Shal it be conseil?**   shall it be a secret (i.e. will you keep it secret)?
  shrewe   scoundrel.

535 **brynge it wel aboute**   bring it about successfully.

537 **I wol thee nat biwreye**   I will not betray you.

540 **whan that he is set**   when he has sat down.
  right anoon   straight away.

542 **ryve**   stab.

543 **strogelest with hym as in game**   struggling with him as if in fun.

544 **looke thou do the same**   make sure you do the same.

547 **oure lustes all fulfille**   fulfil our desires.

548 **at oure owene wille**   just as we please.

549 **acorded**   agreed.

550 **sleen**   slay.
  thridde   third. What light do the events of this section cast on the oath of brotherhood the three revellers swore a short while before?

The revellers kill one another: Lines 551–608

Meanwhile, all the way to town, the youngest of the revellers thinks about the money and how he could get it all for himself. At last the devil puts the thought into his head that he could poison his companions and keep all the money (558). He goes straight to town and goes to an apothecary to buy some poison, telling the apothecary that he wants it to kill some rats and a polecat that has killed his hens. The apothecary gives him a powerful poison that will kill extremely quickly. The young reveller takes the poison, borrows three bottles and puts poison into two of them, keeping the other clean for his own drink. Armed with these bottles, he returns to his friends. When he returns, they kill him just as they had planned. Afterwards they decide to have a drink before burying the body. They both drink from one of the poisoned bottles and die.

552 **rolleth up and doun**   considers in his mind.
554 **if so were that I myghte**   if only I might.
556 **trone**   throne (i.e. no man on earth).
557 **murye**   happily.
558 **feend**   fiend, i.e. devil.
559 **Putte in his thought**   put in his mind.
561 **For-why**   because.
　　 in swich lyvynge   in such a state of mind.
562 **him to sorwe brynge**   bring him to sorrow.
563 **outrely**   completely.
　　 fulle entente   full intention.
565 **tarie**   delay.
566 **pothecarie**   apothecary (seller of drugs and potions).
567 **preyd**   asked or beseeched.
568 **quelle**   kill.
569 **hawe**   yard.
570 **capouns**   chickens or hens.
571 **fayn he wolde wreke hym**   desired to avenge himself.
572 **destroyed**   ruined, injured, or caused damage to.

576 **confiture** concoction or preparation.

577 **Noght but the montance** no more than the amount.
corn of whete grain of corn.

578 **forlete** lose.

579 **sterve** die.

579–80 **in lasse... but a mile** in less time than it would take you to walk a mile. What effect is created through the young reveller's conversation with the apothecary?

582 **yhent** grabbed.

583 **sith** then.

588 **shoop him for to swynke** prepared himself for work.

590 **with sory grace** wretched, accursed.

592 **repaireth** returns.

593 **What nedeth... moore?** what need is there to talk any more about it? (Note how the Pardoner adds impact to his tale by ending it so quickly.)

594 **cast** planned.

595 **anon** immediately.

599 **par cas** by chance.

601 **yaf** gave.

602 **storven** died.

603 **Avycen** Avicenna, a great Arabian philosopher and medical authority who lived in the eleventh century. His writings on medicine were widely known and highly valued.

604 **no canon** one of Avicenna's most important works was called *The Book of the Canon in Medicine*. The term *canon* is often used to mean the rules of procedure.
fen a section of the work.

605 **Mo wonder signes** more strange symptoms.

606 **er hir endyng** before they died.

607 **homycides** murderers. How do you respond to the way the Pardoner ends his tale?

The Pardoner drives home his point: Lines 609–629

Having finished his tale, the Pardoner now moves into the final phase of his routine by exclaiming against the sins of murder, gluttony, lust, gambling and blasphemy. He asks his congregation how they can be so false and unnatural towards their creator (615) – another of his ploys to make them feel guilty enough to come forward to buy his pardons. He urges them to offer him gold or silver coins, but he is also happy to accept goods such as silver brooches, spoons, rings or wool from women. (He can, of course, sell all such items later and so convert them into cash – see his comment in line 162.) He assures the people that as soon as they have parted with their money, their names shall be entered on a roll that the Pardoner carries with him and they will go to heaven. He will use his great power to absolve them of their sins.

- 610 **traytours homycide**   traitorous murder.
- 611 **glotonye, luxurie, and hasardrye**   the Pardoner emphasizes the three sins he set out to attack – gluttony, lechery and gambling.
- 612 **vileynye**   disgraceful conduct.
- 613 **usage**   habit (bad behaviour and swearing from habit).
- 614 **bitide**   happen.
- 615–7 **That to thy... unkynde, allas**   that you are so false and cruel to your creator who made you and redeemed you with his precious heart-blood. How effective do you find the Pardoner's summing up?
- 619 **ware yow fro**   beware of.
- 620 **warice**   heal.
- 621 **nobles**   coins valued at a third of a pound (worth a lot more in Chaucer's time than today).
  sterlynges   silver pennies.
- 622 **silver broches, spoones, rynges**   note that the Pardoner is prepared to take goods if money is not available. This emphasizes that he is interested in gaining as much as possible in whatever form.
- 624 **wolle**   wool (again an item of commercial value to the Pardoner).

625 **Youre names I entre heer in my rolle anon**   the Pardoner
enters the names of those who have been given a pardon on his
'official' list.

626 **Into the blisse of hevene shul ye gon**   another of the
Pardoner's ploys to dupe his gullible audience (but not the other
pilgrims) into thinking that if they pay up they will enter heaven.

627 **assoille**   absolve (of your sins), grant pardon.

628 **clene and eek as cleer**   pure and also as spotless.

The Pardoner tries his persuasion on the pilgrims: Lines 629–682

The Pardoner has finished his 'performance' and now addresses the
pilgrims, telling them that this is how he preaches, and now Jesus
Christ will allow them too to receive his pardon. He urges them to
accept that this is for the best, and that he does not want to deceive
them. He says he has forgotten to mention that he has some relics
in his bag and that if any of them want to come forward and offer
gifts in return for absolution he will be happy to grant them his
pardon. Alternatively, they can be granted a pardon as they travel
along – provided, of course, they offer him money. He points out
that accidents can occur on the journey and so they are very
fortunate to have a pardoner on hand to absolve them of their sins,
in case anyone should fall from their horse and break their neck.

He urges the Host to be the first one to come forward and be
granted pardon. The Pardoner has picked the wrong man here,
though, and he receives, in return, a torrent of obscene abuse from
the Host. The Pardoner is so angry he cannot speak, and in the
end the Knight has to intervene to restore order and persuade
the pair to reconcile their differences.

630 **leche**   healer or doctor (from leeches, which were used in
medical treatment).

634 **male**   bag.

636 **yeven by the popes hond**   given to me personally by the Pope
(the Pardoner again is trying to impress).

637 **of devocion**   out of devotion to God.

639–44 **Com forth... and trewe**   come forth and kneel down here and humbly receive my pardon; or else you can seek forgiveness as you go, new and fresh at the end of every mile, providing that you offer gold coins or pennies that are genuine. (The Pardoner is now trying to 'sell' to the company of pilgrims.)

645 **everich**   everyone.

646 **mowe**   may.

suffisant pardoneer   capable pardoner (note that he is telling them how lucky they are to have a pardoner with them).

648 **For aventures whiche that may bityde**   in case of accidents which might happen.

649 **Paraventure**   perhaps.

650 **atwo**   in two.

651 **seuretee**   security.

653 **bothe moore and lasse**   both high and low (in rank).

655 **rede**   advise.

656 **envoluped**   enveloped.

661 **Lat be**   leave me alone.

662 **breech**   breeches.

664 **with thy fundement depeint**   stained with your excrement.

665 **croys which that Seint Eleyne fond**   St Helena was believed to have found the actual cross on which Christ was crucified.

666 **coillons**   testicles, balls.

667 **seintuarie**   a box for keeping and displaying relics.

668 **Lat kutte hem of**   let them be cut off.

669 **They shul be shryned in an hogges toord!**   they shall be enshrined in a hog's turd.

671 **wrooth**   angry.

674 **worthy Knyght**   the Knight, as the highest in rank of the pilgrims, intervenes to settle what could become a nasty quarrel.

676 **right ynough**   it is quite enough.

679 **yow**   the Knight uses the plural form here as a mark of respect for the Host.

680 **thee**   the Knight uses the singular form here, which signifies a less respectful, more commonplace form of address.

681 **as we diden**   as we did before. Why do you think the Pardoner tries to sell his pardons to the pilgrims after he has just told them all about his true motivation?

Glossary

abhomynable unnatural, hateful, abominable
a-blakeberyed wandering about
aboght purchased
abyde endure (461), wait (477)
abye purchased, paid for
actes histories, records
adoun down
adversarie adversary, enemy
advocatz advocates, counsels
agayn against (141), again, back (431)
agayns in the presence of
agon ago, gone, past
al all
al day always, continually
alestake inn sign
algate however, all the same
alle all
alliaunce alliance
allie ally
alwey always, continually
amende correct, make better, reform
amis wrongly
annexe attach, linked to
anon at once, immediately
apaas slowly
apothecarie pharmacist, seller of herbal cures
artow art thou
aryse arise, stand up
as as if, such as
assaille assail, attack
assent party (472), agreement (515)
assoille pardon, absolve

asterte avoid
atte at the
atwo in two
auctoritee authority
avarice avarice, greed
avaunce benefit, promote
aventure chance, accidents, adventures
avow vow, swear
avyse advise, consider, warn
axe ask
ay always, continually

bad advised, told
baskettes baskets
baudes bawds, procurers of women
beautee beauty
beel amy good friend
been be, are
beestes animals, beasts
beggen beg
bekke nod the head
bely belly
bere bear, carry
berie bury
berne barn
bet quickly
beth be
beye buy
bicched cursed
bicomen become
bidde bid, ask
bifore before
biforn before, in front of
bigynne begin
bihoold behold, see

bisinesse business
bitide happen, come about
biwreye reveal, expose
blame fault
blaspheme blasphemy
blede bleed
blisse bliss, blessedness
blissed blessed
blithe happy, glad
boght agayn redeemed
boke book
bone bone
boon bone
boost boast, boasting
borwe borrow
botell bottle
bourde joke
bowen bow
boyste box
breech breeches
breed bread
breeth breath
breke break
brighte bright, shining
broches brooches
broghte brought
bulle papal bull, edict, document
busshels bushels
but unless
buxom obedient
by close, near (280), by (2), by means of (172), during (572)

cake loaf of bread
cam came
canon see Notes, p. 52, line 604
capitayn captain, commander
capoun capon, chicken

cardynacle see Notes, p. 27, line 27
carie carry
carl fellow, churl
cas, par cas by accident, chance
cast plan
catel property, goods
cause reason
certes certainly, surely
chambre room, bedroom
chaunce chance
chaunge exchange, change
cherl fellow, peasant
chese cheese
cheste clothes chest
cleer clear, clean
clene clean, pure
clepe call, name
clerk scholar, clergyman
clout, clowt piece of cloth
cod bag
coillons testicles
cokewold cuckold; husband of an unfaithful wife
comaund command
commune common (310), general (315)
compaignye company, group
confiture preparation
confusioun downfall, ruin
conseil secret, secrecy
contrarie opposite
contree country, neighbourhood
corny strong, malty
correccioun correction
corrupcioun corruption, foulness
corrupt corrupt, depraved, debased

cors   body, corpse
countrefete   copy, imitate
coveityse   covetousness, greed
crepe   creep
croked   crooked, winding
croys   cross
cure   care, concern
curs   curse
cursednesse   wickedness, evil
  practice
curteisye   courtesy, good
  manners
cut   lots (as in drawing straws)
cynk   five

dame   lady, mother
dampnable   damnable,
  outrageous
dampnacioun   damnation
dar   dare, venture
daunce   dance
debate   contend, attack, quarrel
deceite   deception, deceit
deceyve   deceive
dede   deed, act
deed   dead
deere   dear, beloved (15), dearly,
  at high price (7, 216)
dees   dice
deeth   death
defame   disgrace, loss of
  reputation, dishonour
defaute   fault, sin
deffende   forbid
delices   delights, pleasures
departed   shared, divided
depeint   stained
desolaat   totally disgraced
destourbe   hinder
destroye   destroy, ruin

devel   devil
devocioun   devotion
devyse   invent, devise
deyde   died
deyntee   delicate
diete   diet, food and drink
digne   worthy, honourable
dignitee   honour
discrecioun   discretion,
  judgement
displesance   annoyance
distourbe   disturb, hinder
dominacioun   domination,
  control
dong   dung
doom   judgement
doon   do, cause, bring about
doost   do, make
dooth   does
doun   down
douteless   without doubt
dowve   dove
draughte   draught, drink
drawe   draw, come
drede   doubt
dronke   drunk
dronkelewe   habitually drunk
dronken   drunk
dronkenesse   drunkenness
dyen   die

ech   each
echoon   each one
eek   also
eighte   eight
eir   air
eldre   older
eldres   elders, ancestors
elles   otherwise, else
embassadour   ambassador

empoisonyng poisoning
empoysonere poisoner
endyng end, death
ensamples examples, illustrative stories
entencioun intent, purpose
entente intention
entre enter
envoluped wrapped up, enveloped
er before
erly early
erme grieve, mourn
erst er before
erthe earth
espye spy
est east
estaat rank, social position
eten eat
everich each
everychon every one
expresly definitely, explicitly

fader father
fals false, untrue
famyne famine, hunger
faste close, near
fastynge fasting
fayn willingly, eagerly
feend fiend, devil, Satan
feeste feast, banquet
felawe comrade, companion
felaweship company
felicitee happiness
fen section of a book
fest fist
fetys slim, dainty, shapely
fey faith, word
finden find, discover
flaterye flattery

folwen follow
folye foolishness, folly
fond found
foond found
for because, for
forbedeth forbids
forby close by
fordronke very drunk
forgat forgot
forlete lose
forsweryng perjury, false swearing
forthermo furthermore
forther over moreover
for-why because
forwrapped wrapped up
foryeve forgive
free generous, liberal
freed friend
fro from
frutesteres fruit-sellers (see Notes, p. 39, line 192)
fruyt fruit
fumositee heavy vapour, headiness
fundement dung, excrement
fyne fine, pure
fyr fire

galiones see Notes, p. 27, line 20
gan began
gaude trick
gentil noble
gentils gentlefolk, nobles
giltelees innocent, blameless
gilty guilty
glorie glory, fame, honour
glotonye gluttony
glotoun glutton
golet gullet, throat

good-man master of the house, householder
goon gone
gooth goes
governaunce rule, government
grace favour
graunte agree, grant
grayn grain, seed
greet great, excessive
grette greeted
grettest greatest
grinde grind
grisly dreadful, horrible
grote groat – a coin worth four pennies in Chaucer's time
gytern a musical instrument similar to a guitar

habitacioun dwelling
han have
hadde had
happe happen
harrow cry of distress
hasard a game with dice, gambling
hasardour gambler
hasardrye gambling
haunteden practised, devoted themselves to
hauteyn loud, high-pitched
hawe farmyard
heed head
heere hear
heeste order, commandment
heigh high, great
hele heal, cure
hem them
henne hence
hente take, seize
herkneth listen

herte heart
hewe colour, appearance
heyre made of hair cloth
hir her (84)
hir, hire their (5, 116, 182, 247, 319)
holde keep in memory (152), held (310)
holynesse piety, goodness
homycide manslaughter (358), murderer (607)
honeste respectable, decent
honge hang
honurable honourable
hool whole, healed
hoold keep (176)
hooly holy
hoom home
hoor hoary, white
hoord hoard
hous house
hyne servant, labourer

ich I
idel vain
ire anger

jalous jealous
jalousie jealousy
jape joke, trick
jolitee jollity, happiness, gaiety
joly jolly, merry, lively
juges judges
jurdones chamber-pots
justise justice, law

kaityf captive, wretch, prisoner
kan know, be able
kanstow canst thou
keepe notice, heed

kepe keep, guard, take care of
kisse kiss
knave boy, attendant, servant
knele kneel
knokke knock
knowe know
kyndle kindle, set alight
kutte cut

labour work, toil
lafte left
lasse less, inferior
latoun brass
laughe laugh
leche healer, physician
lecherye debauchery, lust
leef eager (474), leaf (258)
leere learn
leet let, allow, permit
leeve dear
lenger longer
lese lose, forfeit
lesyng telling lies
lete give up, leave, permit
letuarie medicine
leve leave, permission
levere rather, more desirable
lewed ignorant, ill-educated
licour liquor, juice
lige liege, feudal
likerous wanton, lustful
lond land
looke take (for example)
lordynges gentlemen, sirs
lough laughed
luxurie gluttony, lust
lye lie, speak falsely
lyf life
lyk like
lyking desire, wish

lyven live, spend
lyvestow livest thou
lyvynge frame of mind

maister master
maken make
maladye illness, sickness
male bag, wallet
maner kind of, manner
manslaughtre manslaughter
mark mark – a coin worth 40
  groats
mary bone marrow
mateere matter, subject
mayde maiden, girl
mekely humbly
mesurable moderate
mete food (not necessarily
  meat)
miteyn, mitayn mitten, glove
mo more
montance amount, quantity
mooder mother
moore more
moot must
moste must
mowe can
moyste freshly brewed
multiplie increase, multiply
murye, myrie merry
myght power, might
mystriste mistrust

name name, reputation
namely particularly, especially
namoore no more
nat not
nathelees nevertheless
nayles nails
ne not, nor

necessarie necessary, needful
nedeth is necessary
nekke neck
never-a-deel not at all
newe again
nexte nearest
nobles nobles – gold coins
  worth 20 groats
noght not at all, nothing at all
noo don't know
nothyng nothing, in no way,
  not at all
ny nearly

o one
of of (29, 88), from (54, 70,
  122, 163, 650)
officeres servants
offren offer, make offering of
ofte tyme often, frequently
oghte ought
oght us we ought
ook oak tree
oon one
ordre order
otes oats
otherweys in any other way
othes oaths
oures ours
outrely utterly
over over, beyond
overal in addition to
owene own
oweth own, have
oxe ox

paas pace, walking pace
page servant, attendant
paraventure perhaps
par cas by chance

par chaunce by chance
pardee by heaven
parten depart
patente official letter, licence
pees peace, silence
pens pence
peple people
persevereth lasts, continues,
  endures
peyne take pains or trouble
  (44), pain, torment (225)
pitee pity, sorrow, distress
plat plainly
plentee plenty, large amount
plesaunce pleasure,
  amusement
pley play
pleyne complain, lament,
  grieve
plight pledged
pokkes pock marks, pimples
polcat polecat, weasel
policye policy, ruling,
  administration
potage soup, stew
pothecarie apothecary, chemist
povereste poorest
poverte poverty
povre poor
poyson poison
preche preach
predicacioun sermon,
  preaching
preest priest
prelat priest
prey beg, pray
preyde asked
preyere prayer
privee secret, stealthy
prively secretly, stealthily

pronounce announce
propre real, handsome (23) real (131)
proud bold
prow profit, advantage, benefit
pryvee lavatory
pulpet pulpit
purs purse, money bag

quelle kill
quod, quoth said
quyte requite, pay back, punish

rage rage, fury, fit of madness
rather sooner, earlier
ratt rat
receyve receive
rede read (222, 456), red (240, 276), advise (507, 655)
redily quickly, without delay
reed advice, counsel
rekke care
relik relic
renne run
renoun renown, repute
rente tear
repaire return, go back
repente repent
repleet full
reporte relate, repeat
repreeve reproach, shame
reprevable worthy of reproof, shameful
resoun opinion, reason
ribaudye ribaldry, debauchery
rightwisnesse righteousness
riot revelry, debauchery
riotour reveller
rolle roll, document

rolleth consider, turn over in the mind
rote heart, rote, memory
ryde ride
ryve stab

saffron saffron; flavour, colour
sauce sauce
saugh saw
scabbe scab
seel seal of authority
seintuarie casket for relics
seith says
selle sell
sely innocent
semen seem, appear
sepulture grave, tomb
sette sit down
seuretee security
seyde said
seyn say
shoop intended, planned
sholder shoulder
shrewe scoundrel, villain, rogue
signe sign, symptom
sith since (104), afterwards, then (583)
sitte sit
slaw killed
sleen slay, kill
sleeth slays
slyly stealthily, secretly
smale small, slender
smerte smartly, painfully
smoot struck, smote
sobrenesse sobriety
sodeynly suddenly
softe softly, gently
som some

sondry sundry, different, various
soone soon
soor sore
soore deeply
soothe truth
soothly truly
sorwe sorrow
sory sad, sorrowful, wretched
soule soul
soun sound
sovereyn supreme, principal
sowe sow
spak spoke
speke speak
spere spear
spicerie mixture of spices, spicery
spitte spit
staf staff, stick
stampe pound in a mortar
stele go secretly
sterlynges silver pennies
sterve die
stire stir, incite
stirte jumped
stonde stand
stoon precious stone
stoor store, stock
storie story, history, record
strecche stretch
strenger stronger
strete street
streyne strain through a sieve
strogel struggle
strong powerful
stryving strife
styked stabbed, stuck
stynge sting
stywe brothel
substaunce substance, real

nature (see Notes, p. 39, line 253)
subtilly cunningly
suffisant capable, competent
suffyse be sufficient, suffice
superfluytee excess, excesses
swelle swell
swere swear
swich such
swithe quickly
swoote sweetly
sworen sworn
swyn swine, pig
swynke toil, work hard
syde side
synne sin

taak take
talent appetite
tarie delay
t'assoille to absolve, pardon
taverner innkeeper
teche teach
tendre tender
terme formal language, technical terms
thanne then
theech may I prosper
theef thief
theen prosper
theme subject, topic, text
ther there, where
ther biforn previously
thider there, thither
thilke the same
thise these
tho those
thoghte thought, it seemed
thridde third
throte throat

thurgh through
thurghout right through
thynketh it seems
til to
to too
togidres together
tombestere dancing girl
tonge tongue
to-nyght last night
toold told
toord turd
torente tear to pieces
torn turn, show of kindness
totere tear apart
toun town
toweardes towards
traytour traitorous
tresor treasure hoard
trespas sin
trespased sinned against
trespasse do wrong, sin
trete deal with
tretee agreement, treaty, diplomacy
trewe true, genuine, honest
trewely truly, certainly
treye three
triacle antidote, remedy
troden stepped
trone throne
trouthe truth
trowe suppose, think
torne turn, change
tweye two
twinne depart, separate
tyme time, season

unbokele unbuckle
unkynde unnatural, hard-hearted

urinals containers for holding urine
usage habit, custom
useth practises

vanysshe vanish, waste away
venym venom, malice
verray true, truthful
veyne vain
vice vice, wickedness
vicious wicked, vicious
vileynye wickedness (217, 612), rudeness (454)
visage face
voys voice
vyne vine

waferer confectioner, cake-seller
war beware
ware yow beware of
warente safeguard, protect
warice cure, heal
warne warn against
wasshe washed
welked withered
wenche wench, girl
wende go, leave
wende believed, have thought (496)
wenen imagine, believe
weneth imagines
wey road, path
whan when
whennes whence
wher where
whereas where
whete wheat
whilom once (upon a time)
whyl that while

65

wight   person
wikkednesse   wickedness
wille   wish, desire, be willing to
wilfully   voluntarily
wise   manner
wisely   discreetly
wiste   knew
wit   intelligence, wisdom
withouten   without
witnesse on   take as witness
wo   sorrow
wol   will
wolde   wished, would
wolle   wool
wombe   belly, stomach
wont   accustomed
wood   mad
woodnesse   madness
woost   know
woot   knows
worm   snake, creeping creature
worste   worst
worthy   noble
wrappe   wrap
wrecche   wretch
wrecchednesse   misery,
    wretchedness
wreke   avenge
wrooth   angry
wydwe   widow
wyf   woman, wife
wyke   week
wyn   wine
wynne   win, gain

wyn-yevyng   the giving of wine
wyse   wise

yaf   gave
ybore   born
ycaried   carried
ycoyned   coined
ycrammed   crammed, filled
ydel   idle
ydelly   idly, in vain
ye   you (107), yes (406, 579)
yeer   year
yerne   busily, eagerly, rapidly
yeve   give
yeven   given
ygraunted   granted
yhent   seized
yholde   held, considered
yifte   gift
ymaad, ymaked   made
Ynde   India
ynough   enough
yong   young
youthe   youth
yow   you
ypocras   spiced wine
ypocrisye   hypocrisy
yset   seated
yshriven   absolved, shriven
yslawe, yslayn   slain, killed
yspoke   spoken
ystonge   stung
yvel   evil, wicked
ywis   certainly, indeed